ISLAMIC NIKAH BOOK

THE ISLAMIC MARRIAGE GUIDE

ACCORDING TO THE LIFE OF PROPHET MUHAMMAD [PBUH]

BY ISLAMIC BOOK STORE

Published By:
Islamic Book Store
302 Saad Residency
Sahin Park, M G Road
Bardoli, Surat, Gujarat
India
394601
Contact: 0091 9979353876

CONTENTS PAGE

CONTENTS PAGE 1
INTRODUCTION 3
SIMPLICITY 6
IMPORTANCE OF MARRIAGE 7
BENEFITS OF MARRIAGE 8
HARMS OF NOT MARRYING 12
RULING OF MARRIAGE 13
HASTENING OF MARRIAGE 14
BASIS FOR CHOOSING A PARTNER 17
VIEWING THE PROSPECTIVE BRIDE 24
SIMPLICITY IN NIKÂH – EXEMPLARY MARRIAGES 26
SUMMARY 55
THE WALÎMAH 59
CUSTOMS 62
CHRISTIAN CUSTOMS: 66
HINDU CUSTOMS 68
WESTERN, MODERN CUSTOMS 71
OTHER EVILS 74
ACTIONS AFTER MARRIAGE 89
PROHIBITTED ACTIONS 92
ETIQUETTES OF SPOUSES 94

ETIQUETTES FOR HUSBANDS 96
ETIQUETTES FOR WIVES 103
CONCLUSION 109
BIBLIOGRAPHY 110

INTRODUCTION

باسمه تعالى

نحمده و نصلى على رسوله الكريم

قَالَ اللهُ ﷻ وَمِنْ آيَاتِهِ أَنْ خَلَقَ لَكُم مِّنْ أَنفُسِكُمْ أَزْوَاجًا لِّتَسْكُنُوا إِلَيْهَا وَجَعَلَ بَيْنَكُم مَّوَدَّةً وَرَحْمَةً إِنَّ فِي ذَٰلِكَ لَآيَاتٍ لِّقَوْمٍ يَتَفَكَّرُونَ

وَقَالَ رَسُوْلُ اللهِ ﷺ إِنَّ أَعْظَمَ النِّكَاحِ بَرَكَةً أَيْسَرُهُ مَؤُنَةً

All praise is due to Allâh ﷻ alone who created man and women, and, by the institution of marriage, creates a loving and merciful bond between two complete strangers. Salât and salaam upon our beloved master, Rasulullâh ﷺ, who taught us and guided us in marital matters and who serves as a wonderful role-model for us until the Day of Judgement, as well as the sahâbah, tâbi'în, and those who follow their path. Âmîn.

How regretful and pitiable is our condition today that we have cast aside the path of the greatest benefactor to mankind, Rasulullâh ﷺ, and we have aped and adopted the ways of others. Allâh ﷻ declares in the Qurân Karîm, "Most definitely, there is for you in (the life of) Rasulullâh ﷺ a beautiful example, for those who have hope in (meeting) Allâh ﷻ, the Last Day, and who remember Allâh ﷻ in great abundance." If our salâh is in conformance to the salâh of Nabî ﷺ, then it will be correct, otherwise not. Similar is the ruling in our dealings (muâmalât) and manner of living (muâsharât). It is for this reason that Allâh ﷻ did not send an angel as a messenger, but sent a human being, so that he could be a practical example for us. A person whose aim and object is the pleasure of Allâh and who desires success in the Hereafter will take Rasulullâh ﷺ as his role-model and guide. In times of happiness and sorrow, he will not waver from the teachings and path of Nabî ﷺ.

In another verse, Allâh ﷻ declares, "Say (O Nabi ﷺ), if you love Allâh ﷻ, then follow me, Allâh ﷻ will love you and forgive for you your sins. Allâh ﷻ is most Forgiving, most Merciful." The sunnah path is the only way to attain Divine pleasure. Once a person has attained this, Allâh ﷻ will keep such a person happy in this world, in the grave and the hereafter, even though outwardly he may possess little possessions and material means.

In a hadith, Rasulullâh ﷺ is reported to have mentioned, "Whoever holds firmly onto my sunnah at the time of the corruption of my ummah, then for him will be the reward of one hundred martyrs." (Targhib) Hadrat Anas ؓ narrates that Rasulullâh ﷺ said, "Whoever loves my sunnah, then verily he loves me; and whoever loves me will be with me in Jannah." (Tirmidhi) Imâm Mâlik (rahimahullah) said, "Verily the sunnah is like the ark of Nuh ؑ. Whoever boards it, will be saved; and whoever stays back will be drowned."

It has been the habit of my honourable ustadh and sheikh, Hadrat Moulana Abdul Hamid Saheb (dâmat barakâtuhu) as well as my honourable ustadh, Hadrat Moulana Fadhlur Rahmân Azmi (dâmat barakâtuhu) to verbally and practically encourage simple marriages. In fact, the catalyst for writing this book was a desire of Hadrat Moulana Fadhlur Rahmân Azmi (dâmat barakâtuhu) to prepare a booklet on this topic. Therefore, this servant has compiled this booklet on the sunnah method of marriage, since many incorrect ideologies have entered into our marriages. Today millions are wasted in marriage ceremonies, whereas this money could be fruitfully used in so many other noble endeavours. Sins are committed wholesale at such functions, and all vestiges of shame and modesty are thrown aside. Evil is committed in the name of Islam. We lay our complaint to none else but Allâh ﷻ.

May Allâh ﷻ accept this booklet, forgive our shortcomings and make it a means of reviving this sunnah of Nabî ﷺ and the ambiyâ ﷺ, in the whole world till the Day of Qiyâmah.

Moosa Kajee
5 Zul-Hijjah 1431, 12 Nov. 2010, Azaadville

SIMPLICITY

Rasulullâh ﷺ has stated, "Verily the marriage with the greatest barakah (blessings) is that one in which the expenses are the least." (Ahmad/Shuabul-Imân)

Barakah (blessings) in the Arabic language refers to deriving abundance of benefit despite having minimal means. If one desires to achieve happiness, comfort and contentment in life, then this will be achieved through barakah. We are nowadays deceived by external appearances. If a person possesses much wealth, mansions and can fulfil all his desires, he will still never be happy. True enjoyment, comfort and peace of mind will only be attained when we follow the instructions of our Maker ﷻ, who has designed us and knows exactly what is beneficial and harmful for us. By following His commandments, blessings and goodness will ensue.

Hadrat Thanwi ؒ has mentioned that marriage is the easiest of actions. He says, "Regarding marriage, in the shariah, there is so much of comfort, in contrast to the customs which we have invented, in which there is so much of difficulties. See how brief marriage is, that nothing is as brief as it. All other things cost money. In nikâh, one cent does not have to be spent. Money is needed for a house to reside in, and for food and drink, whereas in nikâh not even one cent is needed, because the rukn (fundamental aspect) of nikâh is ijâb (proposal) and qabûl (acceptance). What does it cost to utter these two words? If you say that it costs money to distribute dates and in the mahr, then the answer to this is that it is not compulsory to distribute dates. The mahr (dowry) can be paid at a later time. The main thing from which one cannot escape is the marriage transaction, which costs nothing at all. As for the walimah, it is sunnah, not compulsory. It takes place after the nikâh. Walimah was sunnah in previous times also (i.e. they were very simple). Today most of the customary walimahs are only for show. Money is completely wasted. If we think about it, most of our money is destroyed in ostentation."

Today, unfortunately, marriage has become a curse and burden for many. Millions are wasted, valuable time is lost, and the commands of Allâh ﷻ are openly flouted at such occasions. The time when Allâh ﷻ's special mercy is required, has unfortunately become a source of great enjoyment for Shaytân, who uses this opportunity to cause even pious people to cross bounds and leap into evils which are not ever committed by them. If we desire happiness, blessings, the mercy of Allâh ﷻ, and solace in the home – the actual objects of marriage – then we should endeavour to fulfil this sunnah in the correct way. We have great hope in Allâh ﷻ's mercy that if we try to abide by the life-style of Rasulullâh ﷺ, our marriages and lives will be successful in this world and the hereafter.

IMPORTANCE OF MARRIAGE

1) Hadrat Abu Ayyub ؓ narrates that Rasulullâh ﷺ said, "There are four sunnahs (practices) of the Messengers: a) mehndi (henna) b) itr (perfume) c) miswâk d) nikâh (marriage)." (Tirmidhi)

2) Abu Nujayh ؓ narrates that Nabî ﷺ said, "Whoever possesses the wealth to marry, and then does not marry, then he is not on my path." (Musannaf Ibn Abi Shaibah, Dârimî)

3) Hadrat Anas ؓ narrates that Nabî ﷺ said, "When a slave of Allâh ﷻ marries, then he has completed half his faith, then let him fear Allâh ﷻ in the remaining half." (Shuabul-Imân)

4) Hadrat Abdullah Ibn Mas'ûd ؓ narrates that Rasulullâh ﷺ said, "O assembly of youth, whoever amongst you has the ability should marry. Marriage will help one to lower his gaze and protect his private part. Whoever does not possess the financial ability should fast, since this will break his desires." (Bukhari) The meaning of this is that he should fast for a prolonged period of time, and not just a few days, since this will actually increase one's desires.

5) Hadrat Abû Hurayrah ؓ narrates that Rasulullâh ﷺ said, "Allâh ﷻ has made binding upon Himself the assistance of three people: 1) the warrior in the path of Allâh ﷻ 2) the mukâtab (slave) who wants to pay his due (so that he can be freed) 3) the person who gets married so that he can remain chaste." (Nasai, Tirmidhi)

BENEFITS OF MARRIAGE

1) Children – Hadrat Ma'qil ibn Yasâr ؓ narrates that Rasulullâh ﷺ said, "Marry such women who are loving and

produce children (in abundance) because (on the Day of Judgement) I will vie with other ummahs (and be proud) of your numbers." (Abû Dâwûd, Nasa'i)

The numerical superiority of the ummah will be a source of great pleasure for Nabî ﷺ on the Day of Judgement. Abundance of children is thus a great bounty and has many advantages in this life and the hereafter. After the parent's death, obedient children continuously engage in duâ and acts of reward on behalf of their deceased parents. Children who have received a thorough religious upbringing and Islamic guidance will perpetuate piety and virtue in the future generations. It is mentioned in a hadîth that when the status of a person is increased in *jannah*, he will ask out of wonder: "How did I receive all of this?" (i.e. "How did I receive such a high status when I had not carried out so many good deeds to deserve such a status?") It will be said to this person that this high status is on account of his children seeking forgiveness on his behalf. (Sharhus-Sudur)

Children who died in infancy will be a great aid for their parents in the Hereafter. Through their intercession, the parents will obtain forgiveness and be saved from the calamities of the punishment of Jahannum. It is mentioned that the foetus who is born from a miscarriage (i.e. it is born before its due date) will "fight"(wrangle) with its Creator when its parents are entered into *jahannam*. In other words, this child will go to the extremes in interceding on behalf of its parents and will ask Allah ﷻ to remove its parents from *jahannam*. Through His bounty, Allah ﷻ will accept the intercession of this child and

He will be soft and lenient towards it. It will be said to this child: "O *siqt* (which means, miscarried foetus) who is quarrelling with its Lord! Enter your parents into *jannah*." So this child will draw its parents out of *jahannam* with its navel cord and enter both of them into *jannah*. (Ibn Mâjah)

Pious children who have attained adulthood, too, will be intercessors on behalf of their parents in the hereafter. The greatest benefit in abundance of progeny is the increase in the number and strength of the ummah in this world and the pleasure of Rasulullâh ﷺ in the hereafter.

2) Protection from the plots of Shaytân; controlling of desires, the private parts and the gaze as mentioned in hadith no. 4.

3) Blessings in wealth – Hadrat Aishâ ؓ narrates that Rasulullâh ﷺ said, "Marry women, for they will bring for you wealth." (Bazzâz) If both husband and wife are intelligent, there will be blessings in the income of the husband. The husband will endeavour to earn more because of his added responsibility, while the intelligent wife will not squander the wealth, but will economize and conduct the house budget in a befitting manner. This family will, as a result of this attitude of the marriage partners, become prosperous and this will ensure comfort and peace; which is the very purpose of wealth.

4) Women will take care of the housework, thus allowing the men to earn a living and provide for the family – It is an act of great reward and much significance for a woman to tend to the affairs of her home. Rasulullâh ﷺ exhorted women to do the housework themselves. Once Hadrat Fâtimâ ؓ requested Nabî

for a servant to assist her in her housework. Nabî ﷺ told her, "O Fâtimâ, fear Allâh ﷻ. Fulfil the compulsory duties of your Sustainer and do the work of your house-folk. (Bukhârî, Muslim) A sign of Qiyâmah is that women will leave the confines of their homes and work in shops as narrated by Ibn Masûd ؓ that Nabi ﷺ said, "Before Qiyâmah, salâm will only be made to special people, businesses will spread to such an extent that the woman will help her husband in business, family ties will be broken, false testimony, true testimony will be closed, and the pen will become apparent." (Ahmad, Hâkim)

5) Love in youth and service in old age – Allâh ﷻ declares, "And from amongst His signs is that He created for your benefit from Yourselves partners, so that you may attain solace by her, and He has placed between you love and mercy." Love is found in youth when a man's desires and passions are at a peak. In old age, when desires diminish, Allâh ﷻ places mercy in their hearts so that they serve one another. Even in old age, man needs companionship. It is the height of mercilessness to prevent an old person from remarrying. Many children, in their foolishness, and mostly out of fear of losing a portion of inheritance money, refuse to allow their widowed parents to remarry after their spouse has passed on. This is completely incorrect.

Hadrat Thânwî ؓ writes, "In Shahjahanpur, a man of 90 remarried. His children and daughters-in-law became upset, saying that they would serve him and that there was no need to remarry. He remarked, "What do you know of my needs? None can comfort me like a wife." Sometime later, he became severely ill. He would pass so much of stool that even the area adjacent to him would stink. Not one of his children would even come close to him. His wife, who was of a younger age, and recently married, would purify him and cleanse his clothing, even if he messed 25 times a day. On this occasion, he remarked, "I married for this day." After he recovered, he called for his children and said, "You have seen how much of service you could do. You used to say, "What is the need?" Now you have seen the need. If I did not have a wife, you would have left me and I would have laid here alone."

Besides this, man needs company and solace. In old age, the need for companionship intensifies. By denying him this right, he passes his last years of life in frustration, often thrown around and without happiness. If the father or mother decides to remarry, the children should readily accept this decision, and assist them in whatever way possible.

HARMS OF NOT MARRYING

1) Abstention of marriage will cause one to be deprived of all the above-mentioned benefits. Therefore, it is abominable to refrain from marriage without a valid reason. Reprimanding a wealthy sahâbî, Rasulullâh ﷺ said, "O Ukâf! (while you remain unmarried) you are (like) a brother to Shaytân. If you had been amongst the Christians, you would have become a monk. Our (i.e. Islam's) way is marriage...The worst amongst you are the unmarried. The most effective weapon Shaytân employs

against pious men is women. However, those who are married are saved from immorality." (Ahmad)

2) Nabî ﷺ reprimanded one sahâbî who did not want to marry, saying, "Whoever turns away from my sunnah, he is not from me." (Bukhârî, Muslim)

3) Many evil thoughts and satanic whisperings afflict the mind of unmarried people, which results in the loss of concentration and enjoyment in acts of worship.

RULING OF MARRIAGE

1) Fardh – When one possesses wealth (the minimum being that he works daily and earns enough for the day) and he has such an urgent need to get married, that there is a fear of him falling into prohibited actions (fornication, evil-glancing, masturbation, looking at pornography, etc.)

2) Wâjib – When there is a need and one possesses wealth. By abstention, one will be a sinner.

3) Sunnah – If the need has not reached such a level, and one can fulfil the rights of the wife (sexually and financially)

4) Prohibited – If one possesses a strong fear that he cannot fulfil his wife's rights, whether sexually or monetarily

5) Difference of opinion – if there is a need and one does not have the financial means, then the views differ. According to Hadrat Thânwi ﷺ, in such a situation, it is wâjib (compulsory) to marry. Money can be attained through effort and hard work, or by loans. One should possess a firm intention to repay it and make an effort in this line. Even if one is unable to do so, there is hope that Allâh ﷻ will please the creditor, since the person married for the protection of his religion. However, it is not permissible to take loans for wasteful expenses (like weddings, parties, etc.). This money may be utilized for basic household expenses and for the dowry, where it is demanded immediately.

HASTENING OF MARRIAGE

Nabî ﷺ said, "O Alî, do not delay in three things: 1) salâh when the time enters 2) the janâzah (bier) when it is ready 3) marriage of an unmarried person when a suitable partner has been found." (Tirmidhi)

The word 'ayyim' (unmarried person) can refer to male or female, a person who is a virgin or one previously married. Thus, encouragement is being given to ensure that all members in a Muslim society are married which will place a stop on the evils of fornication which is currently so rampant. How unfortunate it is, that today, many parents delay the marriages of their children, since they feel that they are not old enough, or because of acquiring worldly education. Daughters are married after the age of 25, since they are 'studying'. In the co-ed school and university environments, it is almost impossible for young boys and girls, in the prime of their youth, to control their passions. The chastity of very few youngsters is saved in these environments. Many youngsters who want to save their imân and chastity, and abstain from fornication, then fall into the evil habit of masturbation, which causes great spiritual, medical, sexual, emotional, psychological, and physical harm. Today when even married people are falling into illicit love affairs so easily, then how can parents ever expect their children to abstain and protect themselves? Many parents are in self-delusion that their children will never do such evil. They are living in a fool's paradise. It is very rare to find a young girl who has been to high school and has not been "touched." The minimal is that she will be looked at with desire. Rasulullâh ﷺ has stated, "Allâh ﷻ curses the one who looks and the one looked at." (Shuabul-Imân) After becoming accursed by Allâhﷻ, how can one ever expect goodness from such children?

Many youngsters desire to marry, but parents due to fear of society or other reasons, do not allow it. Many parents will allow their children to date and 'go-out' even feeling proud about this, but when the subject of marriage is broached, they blankly refuse. Instead of some worldly loss or disgrace, man should fear the disgrace of the Day of Judgement, where he will be taken to task for not fulfilling the rights of his children.

Rasulullâh ﷺ said, "Whoever has a child, should give him a good name and teach him noble manners. When he matures, he should get him married. If the child is mature, and the father does not marry him, and the child sins, the sin is upon the father also." (Shuabul-Imân) In another hadith, Rasulullâh ﷺ is reported to have said, "It is mentioned in the Tawrâh, "Whoever's daughter reaches the age of twelve, and he does not marry her, and she commits a sin, then the sin will be upon him." (ibid) Thus the sins of the children, in the form of fornication of the eyes, ears, heart, tongue, hands, or private parts will plummet on the parents. Many young girls abort after falling pregnant, after which her parents are still not prepared to get them married. What answer will they give on the Day of Judgement, when they too will be raised as murderers of innocent children, since they were the indirect cause of this abortion? If a youngster is studying and desires to get married, then his parents should try to make means to support him financially.

Allâh ﷻ states, "If they are poor, Allâh ﷻ will make them wealthy out of His grace." Ibn Abbâs ؓ said regarding this verse, "Allâh ﷻ has encouraged and commanded the free people and the slaves to marry, and promised them wealth. Abu Bakr ؓ said, "Obey Allâh ﷻ in this command of marrying, He will fulfil His promise to you of wealth." Ibn Mas'ûd ؓ said, "Seek wealth in nikâh." (Ibn Kathir) Umar ؓ would say, "I am surprised at the person who does not search for wealth by means of marriage, whereas Allah ﷻ has stated "If they are poor, Allah will make them independent by His grace." (Abdur Razzâq) Rasulullâh ﷺ said, "Allâh ﷻ has taken it upon Himself to aid three persons." One of them is a person who marries to protect his chastity." (Tirmidhi, Nasai)

In the above hadith, Rasulullâh ﷺ made mention of an unmarried person. This includes a widow or divorcee. Unfortunately, this too is regarded as an evil in many societies, whereas it is completely against the grain of Islamic teachings. Due to customs of other societies, especially the Hindus, many people regard it as repugnant and incorrect for a woman to remarry. Many of the former husband's family tell the wife after his demise, "Do not disgrace us by ever getting married." If she remarries, she is regarded as shameless and evil, having brought disgrace to the husband's family. These are customs from the Days of Ignorance, which Nabî ﷺ came to destroy. May Allâh ﷻ save us from such foolishness! Out of Nabî ﷺ's eleven marriages, ten were to previously married women.

BASIS FOR CHOOSING A PARTNER

Hadrat Abû Hurayrah ؓ narrates that Rasulullâh ﷺ said, "A woman is married for one of four reasons; for her wealth, for her family lineage, for her beauty or for her religiousness. Choose the one who possesses religiousness. May your hands be dusty! (Bukhâri, Muslim)

"May your hands become dusty" is an Arabic mode of expression which is used on different occasions. In this context, it is meant to create a yearning and a desire for a pious woman.

Hadrat Anas ؓ narrates that Nabî ﷺ said, "Whoever marries a woman due to her status, Allâh ﷻ will only increase him in disgrace. Whoever marries her for her wealth, Allâh ﷻ will increase him in poverty. Whoever marries her for her family lineage, Allâh ﷻ will amplify his abasement. Whoever marries a woman only intending by it that he may lower his gaze and protect his private part, or to join family ties, Allâh ﷻ will bless him with her, and bless her with him." (Tabrâni in Awsat)

Hadrat Abdullâh ibn Umar ؓ narrates that Rasulullâh ﷺ said, "Do not marry women for their beauty. Perhaps their beauty will lead to their destruction. Do not marry them for their wealth. Perhaps their wealth will cause them to be disobedient. Marry them for their religiousness. A dark-looking slave who is disfigured but is religious-minded is more virtuous (than a beautiful but irreligious woman.)" (Ibn Mâjah)

This in no way means that one should not look for beauty at all. If the circumstances are such that a woman is very pious but at the same time she is so ugly that one's nature does not find her acceptable and there is a fear that if he marries such a woman there will be no mutual understanding between them, and that he will be neglectful in fulfilling her rights, then in such a case he should not marry such a woman.

Man should not marry a woman due to her wealth. This is completely contrary to his self-esteem and honour. It is his duty to earn and support her. It is appropriate to marry such a woman who hails from a family whose material position is equal to or lower than the man. If she is wealthier, then generally she will place high demands on her husband, due to which he will be forced to slave for her. If she uses her money on her husband, then besides rare cases, the man will have to live in humiliation, under her control and rule. The Qurân Sharif explains that one of the reasons Allâh ﷻ has granted man authority over woman is because he spends on her, from his wealth, as this is his duty.

Similarly, family lineage should not be looked at. If the man is from a lower family caste, he will be belittled and regarded as insignificant in the eyes of his in-laws. They will not possess respect for him.

Beauty too, is temporary and short-lived. It can be destroyed with one sickness. After some sicknesses, beauty does not return e.g. at times, one is afflicted with measles or chicken-pox and the marks remain on the face, or the hair falls off. If the object of marriage is wealth or beauty, then as soon as this is removed, all love and affection will end. Hatred will be created in the heart of one another. Besides this, if a woman possesses these traits, but has no piety, then she will generally be conceited and arrogant. She will not care to fulfil her husband's rights. Her object will be to obtain her own rights. No vestige of shame or modesty will be found within her. If the husband possesses some trace of modesty, he will not be able to tolerate her shameless speech and relations with strange men. Excessive beauty could also lead to other more serious sins and vices. Even though beauty is a great bounty from Allâh ﷻ, it can be a means of great destruction. Many men fall in love with women due to their beauty, and end up angering their parents, due to their parents not approving of the marriage. Many such incidents have also occurred where beautiful women got tired of their not so-good looking husbands and thus sought greener pastures.

Note: Marrying on the basis of beauty is the way of the Christians, marrying on the basis of wealth is the way of the Jews, and marrying on the basis of lineage is the way of the polytheists like the Hindus.

The quality which a Muslim should look for in a woman is dîn. This means she should possess Allâh-consciousness, knowledge of the basics of religion and she should be a practising Muslimah. Hayâ (shame and modesty) is the most important quality which should be sought. Today is a time when women are taught to express themselves. This is completely contrary to Islamic teachings. Another quality of vital necessity is that a woman should love to serve her husband. She should know how to cook, run a house and possess love for children. Today many women get married without knowing these basics. Parents flounder in deception that they will learn after they marry. We should remember that if one is not habituated to certain actions during their formative years, then it is extremely difficult for them to thereafter bring within themselves these qualities. It is for this reason that we are commanded to instruct our children to perform salâh when they are seven and to hit them if they are not doing so at the age of ten. When this quality will become a habit at a young age, Insha'Allah, it will always remain. The trend of 'eating out' has come about due to this.

A woman too should look at the religiousness of her prospective partner. She should not concern herself with other unnecessary qualities. Rasulullâh ﷺ said, "When such a person comes to you whose religion and character pleases you, then marry him (to your daughter). If you do not do so, then there will be evil and great corruption in the earth." (Tirmidhi)

Due to the media and other propagation tools, the qualities sought for in partners are exceptionally high and at times ridiculous. Today, many people look for the following qualities:
1) family lineage of Hadrat Hasan and Husein ؓ
2) knowledge of Imâm Abu Hanifah (if religiousness is sought) or Avicenna (if worldly objects are sought)
3) character of Junaid Baghdadi
4) beauty of Yusuf عليه السلام
5) wealth and ruler-ship of Firawn and Qârûn

To find some-one with all these qualities is impossible. If that person's father-in-law had to look for those qualities within him, he would have never married the girl's mother. Similarly, if the girl starts looking for similar qualities in the boy, then it is unlikely any-one will ever marry. Hadrat Thanwi ؓ states that in these times, we should look for the following qualities:
1) There is no doubt in his Islamic beliefs. He does not mock any part of dîn.
2) He has respect for people of knowledge and the pious.
3) He is soft-natured.
4) There is strong hope that he will fulfil the rights of those associated with him.

5) He has enough money to fulfil his necessities, or the strength to earn sufficient wealth.
If such a person comes forward, then one should not delay.

Parents should not make wealth their criterion. Let us ponder over these examples from Islâmic history:

1) Hadhrat Thâbit Bunâni ﷺ narrates that when Yazîd ibn Mu'âwiyâh ﷺ sent to Hadhrat Abu Dardâ ﷺ a proposal for his daughter Dardâ ﷺ, he rejected the proposal. One of Yazîd's companions said, "May Allâh mend your affairs. Will you allow me to marry her?" The man persisted, "Then allow me? Allâh will mend your affairs." "Alright," Yazeed said. The man proceeded to propose and Hadhrat Abu Dardâ ﷺ got him married (to his daughter). The news spread that while Hadhrat Abu Dardâ ﷺ rejected Yazîd's proposal, he accepted the proposal of a poor and simple Muslim and then married his daughter to him. Hadhrat Abu Dardâ ﷺ's comment was, "I did it in the best interests of Dardâ. What do you think would be her condition when (in Yazîd's wealthy household) she has castrated slaves standing over her all the time and when her eyes are dazzled when she sees the (opulent) house? Where will her Dîn be then (when she becomes obsessed with worldly wealth)?" (Abu Nuaym in Hilyah, Ahmad)

2) Shah Shujâh Kirmâni ﷺ abandoned his kingship and adopted sûfism. He had a daughter. Another ruler proposed to her but the father refused. Upon seeing a poor, pious young man offering salât in a beautiful manner, he got her married to

him. When she left her parents' home and came to her husband's home she saw a piece of dry bread which was hidden in a water-pot. Upon seeing this, she asked: "What is this?" The boy replied: "This is the left-over of last night. I have left it so that I may open my fast with it." Upon hearing this, she turned to go. The boy said: "I knew from the very outset that a king's daughter will not be happy with my poverty." She replied: "The king's daughter is not displeased with your poverty, instead, she is displeased that you do not have any trust in Allah. I am surprised at my father who told me that you are a virtuous young man. How can a person who does not place his trust in Allah be virtuous and pious?" This boy began apologizing. She said: "I don't want to hear any apologies. Either I remain in this house or this bread remains here." The boy immediately gave this bread in charity and she remained with him.

Some parents, due to custom, will not allow their younger daughter to marry until the elder one is married, even if a suitable proposal comes for the younger one. The result of this is that at times years pass and both daughters are not married. If perchance the elder daughter eventually marries after many years, if becomes difficult to find a suitable partner for the younger one.

In Tâlimud-dîn, Hadrat Thanwi ؒ has written, "If co-incidentally, any girl has to fall in love with a strange man, then it is better to get them married." The reason for this is that if a man and woman fall in love, but the parents are displeased, and force them to get married elsewhere, then in most cases, the old love-relationship is still maintained after marriage, which eventually brings disgrace, humiliation and heart-ache to the entire family. If love has been created for one another, it is difficult to remove it by force. Forcibly preventing two people in love breeds resentment, rebelliousness and hatred. The end result is an eloped marriage, or illicit sexual contact even whilst married to another.

Islamically, there is nothing wrong for a father to seek a suitable partner for his daughter. In the Qurân we read that Shuaib ﷺ found in Mûsâ ﷺ excellent qualities. He thus proposed to him for marriage to his daughter. Similarly Hadrat Umar ﷺ approached Hadrat Uthmân ﷺ and then Hadrat Abu Bakr ﷺ to marry his daughter. Eventually Nabi ﷺ married her.

VIEWING THE PROSPECTIVE BRIDE

Nabi ﷺ said, "When one of you wants to propose to a woman, then if he is able to look towards (those parts of a woman) which creates desire to marry her (i.e. hands and face), then let him do so. (Abû Dâwûd)

Nabi ﷺ has allowed a person interested in getting married to a certain woman to look at her since this will create love in their hearts, and so that a person notices some physical attraction for his spouse. This does not give men the license to view ten to twenty women, and then decide on one. If one, after investigation, is interested in marrying, then only is he allowed to see her. This too should not be in solitude, since Nabî ﷺ has stated, "No strange man should be in solitude with a woman, except that a mahram be present." (Tirmidhi)

It is not permissible for the boy and girl to sit in seclusion in a room to discuss matters. In actual fact, it is a sign of utter shamelessness that a woman audaciously speaks to a strange man in solitude. Unfortunately, the bier of shame has already left the homes of most people. Many-a-times, other male members of the boy also come to 'view' the girl. This is totally incorrect. How can one expect blessings in his marriage when the commands of Allâh ﷻ are broken so boldly and openly!

If the boy or girl are pleased, then they should make istikhârah. Nabî ﷺ said, "From amongst the good fortune of a person is to seek goodness from Allâh ﷻ." (Tirmidhi) The object of istikhârah is to beg Allâh ﷻ for goodness to ensue from the choice you make. It does not mean that one will see a dream. Whatever one now feels in his heart, he should do. Inshâ-Allâh, there will be goodness therein.

Once a man sends the proposal, the woman should also make istikhârah. When Hadrat Zaynab was sent a proposal by Nabî ﷺ, she did not give an answer immediately, even though there could be no better proposal. She said, "I will consult my Rabb." After istikhârah, Allâh ﷻ performed her nikâh to Nabî ﷺ in the heavens. Thus, even if the proposal is very suitable, a woman should make istikhârah, following in the footsteps of the noble wife of Nabî ﷺ.

Once both parties are pleased, and the woman agrees, then they are engaged. There is no special function to celebrate this. This in fact is a custom, found in Christian and Hindu societies. If one glances at the system adopted by Nabî ﷺ and the sahâbah ؓ, we find that as soon as both parties were pleased, the nikâh would be performed immediately.

Nabî ﷺ said, "O Alî, do not delay in three things:......3) marriage of an unmarried person when a suitable partner has been found." (Tirmidhi)

There would be no delay and wait. Nikâh would immediately take place. For this reason, there was so much simplicity.

SIMPLICITY IN NIKÂH – EXEMPLARY MARRIAGES

Rasulullâh ﷺ has stated, "Verily the marriage with the greatest barakah (blessings) is that one in which the expenses are the least." (Ahmad/Shuabul-Imân)

Let us study a few examples in Islamic history to see the simplicity of Islâmic marriages:

1) Hadhrat Ali ؓ narrates, "When a marriage proposal for Fâtimâh ؓ was sent to Rasulullâh ﷺ, a slave of mine asked, "Do you know that a marriage proposal for Fâtimâh ؓ has been sent to Rasulullâh ﷺ?' When I declared that I did not know, she said, 'Well! She has already received a proposal. What stops you from approaching Rasulullâh ﷺ (and requesting

him) to marry her to you?' 'Do I have anything with which to marry her?' I said. She said, "You only have to approach Rasulullâh ﷺ and he will marry her to you." By Allâh ﷺ! She then continued giving me hope until I went to see Rasulullâhﷺ."

However, when I sat before Rasulullâh ﷺ, I was unable to utter a word out of respect and awe for him. Rasulullâh ﷺ asked, "What brings you here? Is there something you need?' When I remained silent, Rasulullâh ﷺ said, 'Have you perhaps come to propose for Fâtimâh ؓ?" "Yes," I managed to reply. "Have you got anything to give as dowry?" Rasulullâh ﷺ asked. "By Allâh!" I replied, "I possess nothing." "What has happened to the suit of armour I gave you?" he ﷺ asked. I swear by the Being Who controls the life of Ali that the armour was the type made by the Hatma bin Muhârib tribe and was barely worth four (hundred) dirhams. When I informed Rasulullâh ﷺ that I still had it with me, he said, "Then I have handed her over in marriage to you, so send it to her as dowry." This was therefore the dowry of Fâtimâh ؓ the daughter of Rasulullâh ﷺ." (Bayhaqi in Dalâil)

Hadhrat Buraydah ؓ narrates that a group of the Ansâr once suggested to Hadhrat Ali ؓ that he propose for Hadhrat Fâtimâh ؓ's hand in marriage. (When he approached Rasulullâh ﷺ,) Rasulullâh ﷺ asked, "What does the son of Abu Tâlib need?" "O Rasulullâh ﷺ!" Hadhrat Ali ؓ replied, "I wish to propose for the hand of Fâtimâh ؓ, the daughter of Rasulullâh ﷺ." All Rasulullâh ﷺ said was, "*Marhaban wa Ahlan.*" Hadhrat Ali ؓ then left and met with the group of

Ansâr who had been waiting for him. When they asked him what had happened, he replied, "All I know is that Rasulullâh ﷺ said, '*Marhaban wa Ahlan*.'" They said, "Even one of two things Rasulullâh ﷺ gave you is sufficient. He gave you both *Ahl* (a family) as well as *Marhab* (a comfortable home)."

After handing Hadhrat Fâtimâh ؓ over in marriage, Rasulullâh ﷺ said, "O Ali! It is necessary for a *Waleemah* to be hosted after consummation." Hadhrat Sa'd ؓ offered a sheep he owned (for the meat) and the Ansaar collected a few *Saa* of wheat (for the bread). When the night of the consummation arrived, Rasulullâh ﷺ gave the couple instructions to do nothing until he arrived. (When he got there) Rasulullâh ﷺ asked for some water, performed wudhu and then sprinkled some of the water on to Hadhrat Ali ؓ saying:

اَللَّهُمَّ بَارِكْ فِيْهِمَا وَ بَارِكْ لَهُمَا فِي بِنَائِهِمَا

O Allâh! Bless the two of them and bless them in their consummation. (Tabrâni)

Another narration similar to the above, states that the du'â Rasulullâh ﷺ made was:

اَللَّهُمَّ بَارِكْ فِيْهِمَا وَ بَارِكْ لَهُمَا فِي شِبْلَيْهِمَا

O Allâh! Bless the two of them and bless them in their two lion-like sons. (Bazzâr)

A third narration quotes the du'â of Rasulullâh ﷺ as:

اَللَّهُمَّ بَارِكْ فِيْهِمَا وَ بَارِكْ عَلَيْهِمَا وَ بَارِكْ لَهُمَا فِي بِنَائِهِمَا وَ بَارِكْ فِي نَسْلِهِمَا

O Allâh! Bless the two of them, shower Your blessings on them, bless them in their consummation and bless them in their progeny.(Ibn Asâkir)

Yet another narration states that Rasulullâh ﷺ added:

وَ بَارِكْ لَهُمَا فِي شَمْلِهِمَا

...and bless their communion. *(Al Bidâyah Wan Nihâyah)*

Hadhrat Asmâ bint Umays ؓ narrates that after Hadhrat Fâtimâh ؓ was married to Hadhrat Ali ؓ, all that they saw in her house was a straw mat spread out on the ground, a pillow stuffed with the bark of a palm tree, an earthen jug and an earthen mug. (On the night of the marriage) Rasulullâh ﷺ sent a message saying, "Do nothing" or "Do not get close to your wife until I come." When Rasulullâh ﷺ arrived, he asked, "Is my brother here?" When Rasulullâh ﷺ forged bonds of brotherhood between the Sahabah ؓ, he forged his brotherhood with Hadhrat Ali ؓ. Hadhrat Ummu Ayman ؓ, a pious woman who was an Abyssinian and the mother of Hadhrat Usaama bin Zaid ؓ asked in surprise, "O Rasulullâh ﷺ! He is your brother and you have married your daughter to him?" Rasulullâh ﷺ replied, "This (marriage) can take place (despite this type of brotherhood), O Ummu Ayman."

Rasulullâh ﷺ then sent for a container of water, uttered some words and then passed his hands over the chest and face of Hadhrat Ali ؓ. He then called Hadhrat Fâtimâh ؓ who stood by him shivering in her shawl out of modesty. Rasulullâh ﷺ sprinkled some of the water on her and also uttered some words. He then said to her, "I have not failed you in my duty to get you married to the family member I love most." Hadhrat Asmâ ؓ narrates further. She says, "Rasulullâh ﷺ then noticed a figure behind the curtain or behind the door and asked, "Who is that?" "Asmâ," I replied. "Asmâ bint Umays?" Rasulullâh ﷺ

asked. “Yes, O Rasulullâh ﷺ,” I confirmed. He then asked, “Have you come to be of service to Rasulullâh ﷺ (and his family)?” “Yes,” I replied, “because a young girl must have a family woman with her on her first night to take care of anything she might need.” Rasulullâh ﷺ then made such a wonderful du'â for me that it is the one deed that I have most hope in (to deliver me to salvation in the hereafter). Rasulullâh ﷺ then said to Ali رضي الله عنه, “Look after your wife” and as he left, he continued making du'â for them until he disappeared in his room."(Tabrâni)

Hadhrat Ali رضي الله عنه narrates that when Rasulullâh ﷺ got him married to Hadhrat Fâtimâh رضي الله عنها, Rasulullâh ﷺ sent for some water and then gargled with it. Rasulullâh ﷺ then took Hadhrat Ali رضي الله عنه into the room where he sprinkled the water on his chest and between his shoulders and then sought Allaah's protection for him by reciting Surah Ikhlaas and the *Mu'awwadhatayn* (Surah Falaq and Surah Nâs). (Ibn Asâkir)

Hadhrat Ali رضي الله عنه reports that when Hadhrat Fâtimâh رضي الله عنها got married, Rasulullâh ﷺ gave her a blanket, a water bag and a leather pillow stuffed with *Idhkhir* grass.(Bayhaqi in Dalâil)

Hadhrat Abdullaah bin Amr رضي الله عنه reports that when Rasulullâh ﷺ sent Hadhrat Fâtimâh رضي الله عنها to (her husband) Hadhrat Ali رضي الله عنه, Rasulullâh ﷺ gave her a blanket, a water bag and a leather pillow stuffed with the bark of a date palm and *Idhkhir* grass. The couple slept on (half of) the blanket and used the other half to cover themselves. (Tabrâni)

Lessons: The marriage of the queen of both worlds was performed with the greatest of simplicity. There was no engagement party. Neither were sweetmeats given out, nor was any jewellery placed on the neck, as is the custom of Hindus, and nor was any ring placed on the finger, as is Christian culture. After the proposal of Hadrat Alî ؓ, Nabî ﷺ said to Hadrat Anas ؓ to go and call Hadrat Abu Bakr, Hadrat Umar, Hadrat Usmân, Hadrat Talha, Hadrat Zubair and a few other sahâbah ؓ. Those who were easily available and close by were called for the nikâh. There was no special wait for people coming from other places, months of preparation, sending of wedding cards, buying and shopping for months, etc. The nikâh was then performed, despite the fact that Hadrat Alî ؓ did not possess much. Nabî ﷺ himself performed the nikâh.

2) Hadhrat Aa'isha ؓ reports that when Hadhrat Khadîjah ؓ passed away, Rasulullâh ﷺ was still living in Makkah. It was then that Hadhrat Khowla bint Hakîm bin Awqas ؓ the wife of Hadhrat Uthmân ibn Madh'ûn ؓ suggested, "O Rasulullâh ﷺ! Are you not interested in getting married?" "To whom?" Rasulullâh ﷺ asked. She replied, "A virgin if you wish or a previously married woman if you wish." "Who is the virgin?" Rasulullâh ﷺ asked. Hadhrat Khowlah ؓ replied, "She is the daughter of the person you like best, Aa'isha the daughter of Abu Bakr ؓ." "And who is the previously married woman?" Rasulullâh ﷺ asked. "She is Saudah bint Zam'ah ؓ," came the reply, "She has believed in you (as Allâh's messenger) and follows you in your religion." Rasulullâh ﷺ then said to her, "Go and mention my name to them."

Hadhrat Khowlah ؓ went to Hadhrat Abu Bakr ؓ's house where she found Hadhrat Umme Rumân ؓ who was the mother of Hadhrat Aa'isha ؓ, Umme Rumân ؓ," she said, "What tremendous goodness and blessings is Allâh ﷻ about to shower on your family! Rasulullâh ﷺ has sent me to propose for Aa'isha's hand in marriage." Hadhrat Umme Rumân ؓ said, "I would love it, but let us wait for Abu Bakr who is soon to arrive." When he came, Hadhrat Khowlah ؓ said to him, "What tremendous goodness and blessings is Allâh ﷻ about to shower on your family! Rasulullâh ﷺ has sent me to propose for Aa'isha's hand in marriage." Hadhrat Abu Bakr ؓ asked, "Is she suitable for him? She is the daughter of his brother."

Hadhrat Khowlah ؓ reported back to Rasulullâh ﷺ the doubt that Hadhrat Abu Bakr ؓ expressed. Rasulullâh ﷺ said, "Go back and tell him that he is my brother in Islâm and that I am his brother in Islâm (not by blood). His daughter is therefore suitable for me." When she conveyed the message to Hadhrat Abu Bakr ؓ, he said, "Call Rasulullâh ﷺ here." Rasulullâh ﷺ then came and Hadhrat Abu Bakr ؓ got Hadhrat Aa'isha ؓ married to him.(Tabrâni)

Another narration states at the end that Rasulullâh ﷺ told Hadhrat Khowlah ؓ, "Go back and tell him that I am his brother in Islâm (not by blood) and that he is my brother in Islâm. His daughter is therefore suitable for me." When Hadhrat Khowlah ؓ returned with the message, Hadhrat Abu Bakr ؓ told her to wait and then left the house. Hadhrat Umme

Rumân ؓ says that Mut'im bin Adi had requested the hand of Hadhrat Aa'isha ؓ for his son Jubayr and Hadhrat Abu Bakr ؓ had promised it to him. Because Hadhrat Abu Bakr ؓ never broke a promise, he went to see Mut'im. With Mut'im at the time was his wife who was the mother of the boy in question (Jubayr). She however spoke to Hadhrat Abu Bakr ؓ in such harsh terms that the desire to fulfil his promise to Mut'im was forced out of Hadhrat Abu Bakr ؓ's heart.

Hadhrat Abu Bakr ؓ asked Mut'im, "What have you to say about this girl (my daughter? Are you still interested in getting your son married to her)?" Mut'im however turned to his wife saying, "What have you to say?" She turned to Hadhrat Abu Bakr ؓ and said, "It seems that if we marry the boy to her, you will make him irreligious and enter him into the religion you follow." Hadhrat Abu Bakr ؓ again turned to Mut'im and asked, "What have you to say?" Mut'im replied, "You have heard what she has to say (I stand by that)." Hadhrat Abu Bakr ؓ then left them. Allâh ﷻ had removed from his heart the worry for the promise he had made. He then said to Hadhrat Khowla ؓ, "Call Rasulullâh ﷺ here." She then called Rasulullâh ﷺ and when he arrived, Hadhrat Abu Bakr ؓ got Hadhrat Aa'isha ؓ married to him. Hadhrat Aa'isha ؓ was then six years old.

Hadhrat Khowla ؓ then left them and went to Hadhrat Sauda bint Zam'ah ؓ. She said to Hadhrat Sauda ؓ, "What tremendous goodness and blessings is Allâh ﷻ about to shower on you!" "What is it?" Hadhrat Sauda ؓ asked. "Rasulullâh ﷺ

has sent me to propose for your hand in marriage." "I would love to marry him. Go and tell my father about it." Her father was an extremely old man who was unable to even perform Hajj. Hadhrat Khowla ﷺ went to him and greeted him with the greeting of the Period of Ignorance. "Who is there?" he asked. "Khowla bint Hakeem," she replied. When he asked her why she had come, she replied, "Muhammad ﷺ bin Abdullâh has sent me to propose for Sauda's hand in marriage." "What has she to say?" the old man asked. "She would very much like to marry him," Hadhrat Khowla ﷺ replied. The old man then asked her to call for Rasulullâh ﷺ and when he arrived, he married her to Rasulullâh ﷺ.

When Hadhrat Sauda ﷺ's brother Abd ibn Zam'ah returned from Hajj, he started throwing sand on his head (out of remorse). However, after he had accepted Islâm, he remarked, "By my life! I was a real fool the day I threw sand on my head because Rasulullâh ﷺ married Sauda bint Zam'ah."

Hadhrat Aa'isha ﷺ relates further, "When we arrived in Madinah, we stayed in *Sunh* with the Banu Hârith bin Khazraj tribe. When Rasulullâh ﷺ came to our house one day, my mother came to me as I was swinging on a swing suspended between two palm branches. She took me off the swing and neatened my hair which was very short. She then wiped my face with some water and led me to the door. I was out of breath by then and stood there until my breathing had returned to normal.

My mother then took me into the room where Rasulullâh ﷺ was sitting on a seat with several men and women of the Ansâr. My mother closed the door behind me and said, 'This is now your family. May Allâh ﷻ bless you with them and bless them with you." All the men and women then stood up and left. It was then in our house that the marriage was consummated. Neither was any camel nor any goat slaughtered for my marriage until Sa'd bin Ubaadah sent a platter of food which he usually sent to Rasulullâh ﷺ whenever he was with any of his wives. I was then seven years old (however, several more authentic narrations confirm that Hadhrat Aa'isha ؓ was then nine years old)." (Ahmad)

Lessons: Despite the fact that Hadrat Aa'isha ؓ was of such a small age, Rasulullâh ﷺ did not delay in the performance of the nikâh. Due to her small age, the nikâh was only consummated after three years. The walimâh too was very simple. Whatever was available was given.

3) Hadhrat Abdullâh ibn Umar ؓ narrates that Hadhrat Hafsah ؓ became a widow when her husband Hadhrat Khunays bin Hudhâfah Sahmi ؓ, who was a veteran of the Battle of Badr, passed away in Madinah. When this happened, Hadhrat Umar ؓ met Hadhrat Uthmaan ؓ and asked, "If you agree, I can get you married to (my daughter) Hafsah." "I shall think about it," Hadhrat Uthmaan ؓ replied. After a few days, Hadhrat Uthmaan ؓ said (to Hadhrat Umar ؓ), "I have decided not to marry."

Hadhrat Umar ؓ himself narrates further. He says, "I then approached Abu Bakr ؓ saying, 'If you agree, I can get you married to (my daughter) Hafsah.' He however remained silent. This made me angrier than I had been with Uthmaan ؓ but it was only a few days later that Rasulullâh ﷺ proposed for her hand in marriage. After I had married her to Rasulullâh ﷺ, Abu Bakr ؓ met me and said, 'You were perhaps very angry with me when I failed to give you a reply the day you proposed that I marry Hafsah?' 'I certainly was,' I replied. He then explained, 'The only thing that prevented me from getting back to you was that I knew Rasulullâh ﷺ had spoken about (proposing for) her and I could not divulge Rasulullâhﷺ's secret. I would have accepted the proposal had Rasulullâh ﷺ left her.'"(Bukhâri, Nasaî)

Another narration states that when Hadhrat Umar ؓ complained to Rasulullâh ﷺ about Hadhrat Uthmân ؓ (not accepting the proposal), Rasulullâh ﷺ remarked, "Hafsah shall be married to someone better than Uthmân and Uthmân shall be married to someone better than Hafsah." Rasulullâh ﷺ later got Hadhrat Uthmân ؓ married to his daughter (and himself married Hadhrat Hafsah ؓ).(Ahmad, Bayhaqi)

Lessons: Hadhrat Umar ؓ himself sought a suitable marriage partner for his daughter. Thus there is no harm if the father of the girl approaches a boy in which he notices noble qualities. We also learn that a Muslim should conceal his brother's secrets. He should not divulge them.

4) Hadhrat Ummu Salamah ؓ reports that when her *Iddah* had expired, Hadhrat Abu Bakr ؓ proposed for her hand in marriage but she did not marry him. When Rasulullâh ﷺ sent someone to extend his proposal of marriage, she said, "Do inform Rasulullâh ﷺ that I am a woman who is extremely possessive, that I have children and that none of my guardians are present." (When the message reached him) Rasulullâh ﷺ said, "Tell her, 'As for your statement that you are extremely possessive, I shall pray to Allâh to dispel it. As for your statement that you have children, they shall be well taken care of, and as for your statement that you have no guardians present, none of them who are either present or absent shall object to this." (When the message reached her) Hadhrat Ummu Salamah ؓ instructed her son Umar ؓ saying, "Get up and get Rasulullâh ﷺ married." He then got Rasulullâh ﷺ married (to his mother).(Nasaî)

When Hadhrat Ummu Salamah ؓ arrived in Madinah and told the people that she was the daughter of Abu Umayyah bin Mughiera, they refused to believe her. When some of them were leaving for Hajj, they asked her if she wanted to write to her family (in Makkah). She sent a letter with them (by which they managed to confirm who she was) and when they returned, they believed her. This then increased her status amongst them. After she had given birth to her daughter Zaynab (signalling the expiry of her *Iddah*), Rasulullâh ﷺ proposed for her hand in marriage. She said, "Can a woman such as I be married? I am unable to bear children (because of my age), am extremely possessive, and have children of my own." Rasulullâh ﷺ replied, "I am older than you, Allâh shall remove your extreme possessiveness and your children shall be the responsibility of Allâh and His Rasûl ﷺ."

Rasulullâh ﷺ then married her and whenever he came to her, he would affectionately ask, "Where is Zaynab?" This continued until one day Hadhrat Ammâr (bin Yaasir) ؓ took the child away saying, "She (her presence) is preventing Rasulullâh ﷺ from his needs (with his new bride)." During that period, Hadhrat Ummu Salamah ؓ was still breast feeding the child. When Rasulullâh ﷺ came afterwards and asked "Where is Zaynab?", Hadhrat Qarînah bint Abu Umayyah ؓ (Hadhrat Ummu Salamah ؓ's sister) who happened to be there, informed him that Hadhrat Ammaar ؓ had taken her away (so that Rasulullâh ﷺ could have some privacy). Rasulullâh ﷺ then told Hadhrat Ummu Salamah ؓ that he would see her that night.

Hadhrat Ummu Salamah ؓ then put down her leather spread (beneath her grindstone for the dirt to fall upon) and took out some barley grains from her earthen pot. (After grinding the barley) She then mixed the barley with some fat to make a type of porridge for Rasulullâh ﷺ to eat. After Rasulullâh ﷺ had spent the night with her, he said, "You certainly deserve the respect of your family. If you wish, I could spend seven nights with you, but then I would have to do the same for all my other wives."(Ibn Asâkir)

Lessons: Some men, when getting married to widows or divorcees, became unhappy with the mother bringing her children into his house. They at times force the mother to give her children for custody to some-one else. Rasulullâh ﷺ has left for us such an exemplary and beautiful example. Nabî ﷺ would show great affection towards this child. Another amazing point is that Ummu Salamah ؓ cooked food for the Messenger of Allâh ﷺ on the night of the consummation of her marriage. Marriage was not a hindrance to these basic duties. There are blessings when food is cooked at home. Nowadays, the wife does not cook for a long period after her marriage. Food is mostly 'bought out.' There is lack of blessings in this. If after such food is consumed and a child is born, can goodness be expected from such a child?

5) Hadhrat Ismâ'îl ibn Amr reports that Hadhrat Ummu Habîbah bint Abu Sufyân ؓ said, "What I remember well about the time I was in Abyssinia was the arrival of Najâshi's (the king's) messenger. She was a lady called Abraha and was in charge of the king's clothing and oils. She sought permission to enter and when I allowed her in, she said, 'The king says, "Rasulullâh ﷺ has written to me to get you married to him." I replied by saying, "You have given me most excellent news (I accept)." She then said, "The king asks you to appoint someone to hand you over in marriage." I sent for Khâlid ibn Sa'îd ibn Al Aas and appointed him for the task. Thereafter, out of joy for the news she had brought me, I gave Abraha two silver bangles, two silver anklets and every silver toe ring I was wearing."

That evening, Najâshi ؓ invited Ja'far ibn Abî Tâlib and all the other Muslims who were there. Najâshi ؓ then delivered a lecture saying, "All praise is due to Allâh The Supreme King, The Most Pure, The Giver of Peace, The Mighty and Most Powerful. I testify that there is none worthy of worship but Allâh and that Muhammad ﷺ is His Rasul, and the one about whose arrival Isâ ibn Maryam ﷺ had given glad tidings. I wish to tell you that Rasulullâh ﷺ has asked me to marry him to Ummu Habibah, the daughter of Abu Sufyân. I have complied with his wish and am giving her a dowry of four hundred gold coins." He then poured out the coins in front of the people. Thereafter, Hadhrat Khâlid ibn Sa'îd ؓ spoke. He said, "All praise belongs to Allâh. It is He that I praise and from Him do I seek forgiveness. I testify that there is none worthy of worship but Allâh and that Muhammad ﷺ is the servant and messenger of Allâh whom Allâh has sent with guidance and the true religion that shall overcome all other religions even though the polytheists detest it. I wish to say that I also comply with the wish of Rasulullâh ﷺ and hand over Ummu Habîbah bint Abu Sufyân to him in marriage. May Allâh ﷻ bless Rasulullâh ﷺ."

Najâshi ؓ then handed over the coins to Hadhrat Khâlid ؓ, who accepted it (on behalf of Hadhrat Ummu Habîbah ؓ). When the Muslims then started to leave, Najâshi ؓ said to them, "Do remain seated. It has been the practice of the ambiyâ ﷺ to host a meal on the occasion of a marriage. He then sent for the food and the Muslims ate before leaving. (Al-Bidâyah wan Nihâyah)

Hadhrat Ismâ'îl ibn Amr ibn Sa'îd ibn Al Aas reports that Hadhrat Ummu Habîbah bint Abu Sufyân ؓ said, "I saw my husband Ubaydullâh bin Jahash in a dream looking most horrible and hideous. I awoke with a fright and said, "By Allâh! His condition must have changed." That morning he surprised me by saying, "O Ummu Habeebah! I have thought about religion and see no religion better than Christianity. I had been a Christian before entering the religion of Muhammad. I have now reverted to Christianity." "By Allâh!" I exclaimed, "There is no good for you in this." When I informed him about my dream, he simply ignored it and then got hooked on wine until he died."

Continuing her narration, Hadhrat Ummu Habeebah ؓ says, "I then saw someone in a dream addressing me with the title of 'Ummul Mu'mineen'. I awoke with a start and interpreted the dream to mean that Rasulullâh ﷺ would soon marry me. As soon as my *Iddah* had expired, I well recall when the messenger of Najaashi ؓ came to me..." The rest of the narration is like the one above. The narration however adds at the end that Hadhrat Ummu Habeebah ؓ said, "After the Muslims had eaten and left and the money came to me, I sent for Abraha ؓ who had brought me the good news. I said to her, 'I gave you what I did that day only because I had no money then. Here are fifty gold coins. Please take it and use it for yourself.' She however produced a box containing everything I had given her. Returning it to me, she said, 'The king made me promise that I shall not take anything from you as long as I am in charge of his clothing and oils. I am also a follower of the religion of Rasulullâh ﷺ and have submitted to Allâh ﷻ. The king has already instructed his wives to send to you all the perfumes they have in their possession.' The next morning, she brought me plenty of fragrances such as *Ood, Waras, Amber* and *Zabaad*. I brought back all of this to Rasulullâh ﷺ and although he saw it with me and saw me wearing it, he never objected.

Abraha ؓ then said to me, 'My only request to you is that you convey my Salaams to Rasulullâh ﷺ and that you inform him that I have become a follower of his religion. She treated me very kindly and even helped me prepare for the journey. Whenever she came to me, she would say, 'Do not forget my request.' When I got to Rasulullâh ﷺ and informed him about the proposal and the behaviour of Abraha ؓ, he merely smiled and when I conveyed her salâms to him, he replied by saying:

وَ عَلَيْهَا السَّلَامُ وَ رَحْمَةُ اللهِ وَ بَرَكَاتُهُ

May Allâh's peace, mercy, and blessings be on her. (Hâkim)

6) Hadhrat Anas ؓ reports that when the *iddah* of Hadhrat Zaynab bint Jahash ؓ had expired, Rasulullâh ﷺ told Hadhrat Zaid ؓ to ask her if she would marry him. When Hadhrat Zaid ؓ saw her as she was kneading dough, her status soared so much in his heart because Rasulullâh ﷺ wanted to marry her and that he was unable to even look at her (note: this incident took place before the laws of hijâb were revealed). He therefore turned on his heels and facing his back to her, said, "O Zaynab! Glad tidings to you! Rasulullâh ﷺ has sent me to propose for your hand in marriage." Hadhrat Zaynab ؓ replied by saying, "I am unable to do anything until I consult with my Sustainer." She then stood at the place where she performed her salâh (and engaged in salâh). It was then that Allâh ﷻ revealed some verses of the Qur'ân (in which Allâh ﷻ states,

"We married her (Zaynab) to you (O Rasulullâh ﷺ)..." (Ahzâb)
(Because Allâh ﷻ had conducted the marriage), Rasulullâh ﷺ then went to Hadhrat Zaynab ؓ without needing to seek permission.

Hadhrat Anas ؓ says further, "I was also there when Rasulullâh ﷺ went to Hadhrat Zaynab ؓ and fed us bread and meat to celebrate the occasion. While some people (ate and) left, others remained behind in the room to talk after eating. Rasulullâh ﷺ left the room and I followed him. He then visited the rooms of all his wives to greet them and they all asked him how he found his new bride. I cannot remember if it was I or someone else who informed Rasulullâh ﷺ that the guests had all left, upon which he went back (to Hadhrat Zaynab ؓ's room). As I was about to enter with Rasulullâh ﷺ, he drew a curtain between himself and me because the verses of hijâb had just been revealed. Also revealed was the verse teaching etiquette to the people, which states:

يَا أَيُّهَا الَّذِينَ آمَنُوا لَا تَدْخُلُوا بُيُوتَ النَّبِيِّ إِلَّا أَن يُؤْذَنَ لَكُمْ إِلَى طَعَامٍ غَيْرَ نَاظِرِينَ إِنَاهُ وَلَكِنْ إِذَا دُعِيتُمْ فَادْخُلُوا فَإِذَا طَعِمْتُمْ فَانتَشِرُوا وَلَا مُسْتَأْنِسِينَ لِحَدِيثٍ إِنَّ ذَلِكُمْ كَانَ يُؤْذِي النَّبِيَّ فَيَسْتَحْيِي مِنكُمْ وَاللَّهُ لَا يَسْتَحْيِي مِنَ الْحَقِّ وَإِذَا سَأَلْتُمُوهُنَّ مَتَاعًا فَاسْأَلُوهُنَّ مِن وَرَاءِ حِجَابٍ ذَلِكُمْ أَطْهَرُ لِقُلُوبِكُمْ وَقُلُوبِهِنَّ وَمَا كَانَ لَكُمْ أَن تُؤْذُوا رَسُولَ اللَّهِ وَلَا أَن تَنكِحُوا أَزْوَاجَهُ مِن بَعْدِهِ أَبَدًا إِنَّ ذَلِكُمْ كَانَ عِندَ اللَّهِ عَظِيمًا

O you who have Imaan! Enter the rooms of the Nabi ﷺ only when you are permitted to do so (invited) to partake of a meal. Then too, do not wait for it (the meal) to be prepared (by arriving too early or without invitation), but enter when (the meal is done and) you are called (to eat) and disperse (depart) once you have eaten without (remaining behind and) enjoying a (lengthy) conversation. Indeed this (arriving too early and remaining behind afterwards) hurts the Nabi ﷺ, but he is shy for you (he does not tell you lest you feel offended). (However,) Allâh ﷻ does not shy away from the truth (and makes it clear to all without exception). When you ask them (Rasulullâh ﷺ's wives) for anything, then ask them from behind a curtain (without seeing them). This is purer for your hearts and for their hearts (for it safeguards you from evil thoughts and desires). It is not (permissible) for you (believers) to hurt the Nabi ﷺ (in any way), nor to ever marry his wives after him (after he passes away). Verily this (hurting Rasulullâh ﷺ and marrying his wives after his demise) is grave in the sight of your Rabb. (Ahzâb) (Ahmad, Nasaî, Muslim)

In another narration, Hadhrat Anas ؓ states, "To celebrate his marriage to Hadhrat Zaynab bint Jahash ؓ, Rasulullâh ﷺ hosted a meal of bread and meat. I was sent to invite the people to the meal and as they arrived, they ate and then left. When I could find no one more to invite, I submitted, 'O Nabî of Allâh ﷺ! I cannot find anyone else to invite.' Rasulullâh ﷺ then gave the instruction for the food to be taken away but there were still three people who stayed behind to talk. Rasulullâh ﷺ therefore left the room and went to the room of Hadhrat Aa'isha ؓ. When he greeted her with the words:

السَّلَامُ عَلَيْكُم أَهْلَ الْبَيْتِ وَ رَحْمَةُ اللهِ وَ بَرَكَاتُهُ

she replied by saying:

وَ عَلَيْكَ السَّلَامُ وَ رَحْمَةُ اللهِ وَ بَرَكَاتُهُ

She then asked, "How did you find your wife? May Allâh bless you!" Rasulullâh ﷺ then went to each of his wives' rooms in turn. As he greeted them in the manner he greeted Hadhrat Aa'isha ؓ, they said to him what Hadhrat Aa'isha ؓ had said.

When Rasulullâh ﷺ returned to the room (of Hadhrat Zaynab ؓ), he found the three men still sitting there and talking. Because Rasulullâh ﷺ was extremely bashful, (rather than telling them to leave) he again walked off towards the room of Hadhrat Aa'isha ؓ. I cannot recall whether it was someone else or I who informed him that the men had left. He then returned and his one foot was still on the threshold and the other outside when he dropped the curtain between himself and me, and the verse of hijâb was revealed." (Bukhâri)

Lessons: In all the marriages of Nabî ﷺ, the walimah was extremely simple. It was only in this marriage that extra was prepared as the nikâh was performed in the heavens. Despite the huge numbers of people coming for this meal, they were all fed at home in turns. There was no hiring of halls, caterers, etc. This is not the way of Nabî ﷺ and our pious predecessors. As far as possible, we should hold firmly onto their path.

7) Hadhrat Anas ؓ reports that when the prisoners captured after the Battle of Khaybar were mustered together, Hadhrat Dihya ؓ approached Rasulullâh ﷺ with a request. "O Rasulullâh ﷺ!" he said, "Give me a slave woman from the captives." "Go and take one," Rasulullâh ﷺ said. Hadhrat Dihya ؓ proceeded to take Safiyya bint Huyay. Someone then came to Rasulullâh ﷺ saying, "O Nabî of Allâh ﷺ! You have given to Dihya Safiyya bint Huyay who is the leader of the Banu Qurayzah and Banu Nadhîr tribes! She is suitable only for you." Rasulullâh ﷺ then sent for her and when he saw her, he instructed Hadhrat Dihya ؓ to take another woman. Rasulullâh ﷺ then set her free and married her. (Bukhâri, Muslim, Abu Dawûd)

Hadhrat Anas ؓ narrates that they marched to Khaybar and after conquering the fortress there, Rasulullâh ﷺ was informed about Safiyya bint Huyay bin Akhtab. She was an extremely beautiful lady whose husband had been killed while she was still a new bride. Rasulullâh ﷺ chose (to marry) her and (after leaving Khaybar) it was only when they reached the boundary of *Sahbaa* that she stopped menstruating. It was therefore only there that Rasulullâh ﷺ was able to consummate the marriage. Rasulullâh ﷺ then had some *Hais* (A sweet dish prepared with dates, butter and flour) prepared and served on a leather tablecloth. Hadhrat Anas ؓ was then instructed to invite whoever was in the area (to partake of the food). This was the *Waleemah* meal for Rasulullâh's ﷺ marriage to Hadhrat Safiyya bint Huyay ؓ. Hadhrat Anas ؓ reports further that on the way back to Madinah, he saw Rasulullâh ﷺ use a shawl to make a screen for her behind him. He would then kneel beside his camel and place his knee upright for her to step on as she mounted the camel. (Bukhâri)

Hadhrat Anas ؓ states, "Rasulullâh ﷺ camped at a place between Khaybar and Madinah for three days. It was here that he consummated his marriage to Safiyya ؓ, after which I invited the Muslims present there to a *Walîmah* meal that featured neither bread nor meat. All that it consisted of was Rasulullâh ﷺ's instruction to Bilâl ؓ to spread out a leather tablecloth. He then scattered some dates, cheese and butter onto it (which the people ate). Some of the Muslims asked, 'Is she one of the *Ummahaatul Mu'mineen* (wives of Rasulullâh ﷺ) or his slave woman?' Others replied, 'If Rasulullâh ﷺ veils her, she is one of the *Ummahaatul Mu'mineen*, otherwise she is his slave woman.' When the army started to leave, Rasulullâh ﷺ spread something behind him (for her to sit on) and then pulled a veil over." (Bukhâri)

Hadhrat Jaabir ؓ reports, "When Safiyya bint Huyay bin Akhtab ؓ entered Rasulullâh ﷺ's tent (as his wife), many people including myself presented ourselves there to have a share (of the *Waleemah* food). When he emerged from the tent, Rasulullâh ﷺ said, "Leave your mother (my wife) alone" (they all therefore left). When we gathered at the time of Ishâ, Rasulullâh ﷺ came out to us carrying in the edge of his shawl close to one and a half *Mudd* (A unit of weight used by the Arabs during those times) of Ajwah dates. (Handing them over to us) Rasulullâh ﷺ said, 'Eat from the *Walîmah* of your mother.'" (Ahmad)

8) Hadhrat Aa'isha ؓ narrates that when the captives of the Banu Mustaliq tribe were distributed (amongst the Muslim army), Hadhrat Juwayriyyah bint Hârith ؓ happened to fall in the lot of Hadhrat Thâbit bin Qais bin Shammâs ؓ or one of his nephews. (Rather than being a conventional slave) Hadhrat Juwayriyyah ؓ entered into a contract of *Kitâbah* with him. She was an extremely pleasant and beautiful woman who attracted anyone who saw her. Hadhrat Aa'isha ؓ says, "She one day came to Rasulullâh ﷺ to seek assistance with paying off her *Kitâbah*. By Allâh! I disliked her as soon as I saw her standing at the door of my room because I knew that Rasulullâh ﷺ would also see in her what I saw. When she entered the room, she said, "O Rasulullâh ﷺ! I am Juwayriyyah, the

daughter of Hârith bin Abu Dirâr, the leader of his tribe. As you well know, a calamity has befallen me (when I was captured and taken as a slave). I fell to the lot of Thâbit bin Qais bin Shammâs and entered into a contract of *Kitâbah* with him. I have now come to seek your assistance to pay of the *Kitâbah*.'" (Note: *Kitâbah* is a contract between slave and master by which the slave has to gradually pay the master a certain sum of money to secure freedom.)

"Do you not want something better?" Rasulullâh ﷺ asked. "What is that, O Rasulullâh ﷺ?" she wanted to know. Rasulullâh ﷺ said, "That I should pay off your *Kitâbah* and then marry you." "Certainly, O Rasulullâh ﷺ!" she replied, "I am most willing."

When the news reached the Sahabah ؓ that Rasulullâh ﷺ had married Hadhrat Juwayriyyah ؓ, they said, "They (the tribe of Hadhrat Juwayriyyah ؓ) are now the in-laws of Rasulullâh ﷺ, so free those of them whom you own (as your slaves)." Hadhrat Aa'isha ؓ says, "It was therefore as a result of Rasulullâh ﷺ's marriage to Juwayriyyah ؓ that a hundred families of the Banu Mustaliq tribe were set free. I do not know of any woman who was a greater blessing for her tribe than Juwayriyyah ؓ." (Hâkim, Ibn Ishâq)

Hadhrat Urwa ؓ reports that Hadhrat Juwayriyyah bint Hârith ؓ said, "Three days before the arrival of Rasulullâh ﷺ, I dreamt that the moon came from Yathrib and fell into my lap. I however did not want to tell anyone about this until Rasulullâh ﷺ actually arrived. When we were taken captive, the dream gave me hope and Rasulullâh ﷺ eventually set me free and married me. By Allâh! I never spoke to Rasulullâh ﷺ about (freeing) the people of my tribe until the Muslims freed them by themselves. In fact, I only found out about it when one of my cousins informed me about it. I then praised Allâh for it."(Hâkim, Wâqidi)

9) Hadhrat Ibn Shihaab narrates that it was the year after signing the Treaty of Hudaybiyyah that Rasulullâh ﷺ left to perform Umrah. This occurred seven years after the Hijrah during the month of Dhul Qa'dah, which was the same month in which the polytheists had prevented Rasulullâh ﷺ from entering the Masjidul Haraam (the previous year). When he reached a place called Ya'jij, Rasulullâh ﷺ sent Hadhrat Ja'far bin Abu Taalib ؓ to propose on his behalf for the hand of Hadhrat Maymûnah bint Hârith bin Hazan Aamiriyyah ؓ in marriage. Hadhrat Maymûnah ؓ handed over her affairs to Hadhrat Abbâs bin Abdul Muttalib ؓ who was married to her sister Ummul Fadhl ؓ. Hadhrat Abbâs ؓ then handed her over in marriage to Rasulullâh ﷺ. Rasulullâh ﷺ stayed over in Sarif for a while until Hadhrat Maymûnah ؓ arrived there and the marriage was consummated. Allâh had decreed that Hadhrat Maymûnah ؓ should pass away at the same place where her marriage to Rasulullâh ﷺ was consummated. (Hâkim)

Another narration states that after marrying Hadhrat Maymûnah bint Hârith ؓ, Rasulullâh ﷺ stayed in Makkah for three days. On the third day, Huwaytib bin Abdul Uzza came to Rasulullâh ﷺ with a few men of the Quraysh and said, "Your stay has expired, so leave us." Rasulullâh ﷺ said to them,

"What harm will it do to you if you leave me to consummate my marriage in your midst, after which I shall host a meal which you all can attend?" "We have no need for your food," they snapped, "do leave us." Rasulullâh ﷺ therefore left Makkah Mukarramah with Hadhrat Maymûnah ؓ and consummated his marriage at Sarif. (Hâkim)

9) Hadhrat Rabee'ah ؓ says, "I was Rasulullâh ﷺ's servant. One day he asked, 'O Rabee'ah! Are you not interested in getting married?' I replied, 'I have no intention of marrying. While I have nothing with which to support a wife, I also do not want anything to preoccupy me from (serving) you.' When Rasulullâh ﷺ turned away from me, I said to myself, 'By Allâh! Rasulullâh ﷺ definitely knows better than me what is best for me in this world and in the hereafter. By Allâh! Should he ever again ask me whether I am interested in getting married, I shall reply, 'Certainly, O Rasulullâh ﷺ! Instruct me as you please.' When Rasulullâh ﷺ did ask me whether I was interested in getting married, I replied, 'Certainly, O Rasulullâh ﷺ! Instruct me as you please.' Rasulullâh ﷺ then instructed me to go to a particular tribe of the Ansâr who did not frequently meet with Rasulullâh ﷺ. He told me to tell them that he had sent me to them with instructions to get me married to a certain girl from amongst them. I therefore went to them and informed them that Rasulullâh ﷺ had sent me with instructions that they get me married. "Welcome to Rasulullâh ﷺ and the messenger of Rasulullâhﷺ!" they cried out, "By Allâh! The messenger of Rasulullâhﷺ shall never return without having his need fulfilled." They then got me married and treated me exceptionally well without even asking for a witness.

I returned depressed to Rasulullâh ﷺ saying, 'O Rasulullâh ﷺ! I have been to people who are extremely generous. They got me married and treated me exceptionally well without even asking for a witness. However, I have no dowry to give. Rasulullâh ﷺ then called for Buraydah Aslami ؓ (the leader of my tribe) and instructed him to collect some gold for me equivalent to the weight of a date stone. When I took possession of what the people collected for me, I brought it to Rasulullâh ﷺ who said, 'Take this to them and tell them that this is her dowry.' When I did so and told them that this was her dowry, they accepted it with great happiness and said, 'This is excellent and so much!'

When I again returned depressed to Rasulullâh ﷺ, he asked, "Why so gloomy, O Rabee'ah?" "O Rasulullâh ﷺ!" I began, "I have never met people as wonderful as them. They were happy with what I gave them and treated me extremely well. They even told me that the dowry was excellent and so much." However, I have nothing with which to host a *Walîmah*. "O Buraydah!" Rasulullâh ﷺ called out, "Collect (money) for a goat for him." After the people (of my tribe) had collected (enough to buy) a large and fat sheep, Rasulullâh ﷺ instructed me to go to Aa'isha ؓ and tell her to give me the basket containing the grains. I did as I was ordered and she said, "Here is the basket containing seven *Saa* of barley. By Allâh! By Allâh! We have no other food besides this. You may have it." I took the basket to Rasulullâh ﷺ and informed him about what Aa'isha ؓ had said. Rasulullâh ﷺ said, "Take this to them (your in-laws) and tell them to bake this (the barley) into bread and to cook that (the sheep)." (When I took it to them) They said, "While we can take care of the bread for you, you will have to see to the sheep for us." Some men of the Aslam tribe and I took the sheep, slaughtered it, skinned it and then cooked it. We then had bread and meat with us and I hosted the *Walîmah*. I also invited Rasulullâh ﷺ. (Ahmad, Tabrâni)

10) Hadhrat Salmân Fârsi ؓ reports that he once married a woman from the Kindah tribe and consummated the marriage in her house. On the night of the marriage, his friends walked with him to her house and when they reached it, he said to them, "You may return now. May Allâh ﷻ reward you." He did not allow them to enter the house as foolish people generally do. When he looked at the house which had been decorated (with drapes on all sides), he remarked, **"Is your house feverish (because of which you had to bandage it) or has the Kabah been moved to the Kindah tribe?"** The people replied, "Neither is the house feverish nor has the Kabah been moved to the Kindah tribe." Hadhrat Salmân ؓ then refused to enter the house until all the drapes were removed except for the drape covering the entrance.

When Hadhrat Salmân ؓ finally entered the house, he saw a large amount of goods there. "Whose goods are these?" he asked. "Yours and your wife's," the people replied. Hadhrat Salmân ؓ said, "This does not conform to the advice my beloved friend (Rasulullâh ﷺ) gave me. My beloved friend ﷺ advised me to have only that much of worldly goods that a traveller has as provisions." When he saw a few (female) servants, he asked, "Whose servants are these?" When he was informed that the servants also belonged to him and his wife, he said, "This also does not conform to the advice my beloved friend ﷺ gave me. He advised me to keep only those (female) servants whom I can marry or who I can get married (to others). If I do keep them and they fornicate (because they have none to satisfy their needs), their sins will be on me without any reduction to the sin they will be guilty of."

Hadhrat Salmân ؓ then turned to the women around his wife and said, "Will you ladies leave me to be alone with my wife?" They readily agreed and left. Hadhrat Salmân ؓ then went to the door, shut it and drew the drape over it. Thereafter, he sat with his wife, held her forelock, and made du'â for blessings. He then asked her, "Will you obey any instructions I give you?" Her reply was, "You are sitting in the position of a person who has to be obeyed." He continued to say, "My beloved friend ﷺ advised me that when I meet with my wife (for the first time), I should meet with her in the obedience of Allâh." He then got up and proceeded to the place of salâh with her following him. After performing salâh for some time, they left the place of salâh and he then fulfilled with her the need a man has with his wife.

Early next morning his friends came to him asking, "How did you find your wife?" When he ignored them, they repeated the question. Again he ignored them but again they repeated themselves. When they repeated the question a third time, he ignored them yet again but then finally said, "Allâh has made drapes, curtains and doors to conceal what lies behind them. It is sufficient to ask about things that are apparent but one should never ask about things that are hidden. I heard Rasulullâh ﷺ say that those persons who narrate such (private) things are like donkeys having intercourse on the street."(Abu Nuaym in Hilyah)

Lessons: A person should commence his marriage life in the obedience of Allâh ﷺ. When a man meets his wife for the first time, he should recite the duâ, and both of them should engage in salâh and duâ before consummating their marriage. In this incident as well as many above, consummation would take place in the husbands or wife's houses. There was no hotel, honeymoon, etc.

11) Hadhrat Thâbit Bunâni reports that Hadhrat Abu Dardâ ؓ once went with Hadhrat Salmân Fârsi ؓ to extend a proposal on his behalf for a woman of the Banu Layth tribe. Hadhrat Abu Dardâ ؓ went in to see the family and told them in detail that Hadhrat Salmân ؓ was one of the early Muslims and also recounted his acceptance of Islâm. He then proceeded to mention to them that Hadhrat Salmân ؓ wished to marry a particular girl of their family. Their reply was, "While we do not wish to get Salmân ؓ married (to our daughter), we wouldn't mind getting you married (to her)." They then handed her over in marriage to him and he left.

(When he met Hadhrat Salmân ؓ) Hadhrat Abu Dardâ ؓ said, "Something has happened that I am too embarrassed to tell you about." "What is it?" Hadhrat Salmân ؓ asked. When Hadhrat Abu Dardâ ؓ related the incident to him, Hadhrat Salmân ؓ said, "I should be the one embarrassed since I proposed for a woman whom Allâh ﷻ had destined for you." (Abu Nuaym in Hilyah, Tabrâni)

Subhânallah! Look at the clean hearts the Sahâbah ؓ possessed!

SUMMARY

From all the above-mentioned incidents, it can be clearly seen how simple the marriages were in the era of Nabî ﷺ. A few points to be noted:

A) After acceptance of proposal, there was no delay in the nikâh (marriage). Rasulullâh ﷺ said, "O Alî, do not delay in three things 1) salâh when the time enters 2) the janâzah (bier) when it is ready 3) marriage of an unmarried person when a suitable partner has been found." (Tirmidhi) After having found a partner, we should hasten in conducting the Nikah. Abu Hurairah ؓ narrates that Nabi ﷺ said, "When you receive a proposal from a person who is pious and has good habits, then get your daughters married to them. If you do not do so, it will result in the spreading of evil and corruption." (Tirmidhi)

It has become a habit in some cultures to prolong the Nikah after the engagement; thus, the boy and the girl start meeting each other, or talking to each other on the phone, or chatting online. All of these are not permissible, as an engagement is only a promise to marry and the boy and girl still remain non-mahram (strangers) to each other.

There are many harms of delaying the nikâh:

1) It is only natural that once a boy and girl are proposed, thoughts for one another are created in the mind. Since they are strangers, to volitionally bring thoughts of the other party is fornication of the mind and thoughts. How sad if one commences one's marriage life with this form of fornication!

2) In many cases, the boy and girl meet each other, spend time in solitude with each other, or at the very least, speak to each other telephonically, many-a-time with the blessings of the parents. Fornication of the ears, eyes, hands and feet all occur before the marriage. How can one then draw Allâh ﷻ's special mercy and derive blessings in one's marriage?

3) Shaytân sows doubt in the heart of those to be married, especially the girl. Many times, she falls into so much confusion that she demands that her proposal be broken, thus causing anguish to both parties.

4) Delaying of nikâh is contrary to the way of our beloved Nabî ﷺ as well as his instruction to hasten with marriage.

5) When there is a lot of time before the nikâh, then there is enough time to become extravagant, invite many people, have many parties and ceremonies days before, etc. If the nikâh is performed immediately, then all these evil and unnecessary practices will terminate.

B) If for some reason, the boy and girl cannot live together immediately, then too the nikâh should be performed. The bride can then live with her husband after some time. Hadhrat Ayesha ؓ was only six when she accepted her proposal. Nikâh was immediately performed, even though she began living with Nabî ﷺ when she matured, three years later. Hadrat Umme

Habîbah ؓ was in Abyssinia, when she accepted her proposal. Nabî ﷺ did not wait for her to even return to Medinah Munawwarah, but married her by appointing Najâshi to perform the nikâh on his behalf. Hadrat Safiyyâh ؓ was married whilst she was in a state of menses. The nikâh was performed immediately, and it was consummated after she attained purity, followed by the walimah. On - route for umratul-qadâ in the 7th year hijri, Nabî ﷺ proposed for Hadrat Maymûnah ؓ. When the proposal was accepted, Nabî ﷺ immediately performed the nikâh even though he was in the state of ihram. After performing the umrâh, Nabî ﷺ asked for an extension so that he could consummate his marriage. This was rejected. Nabî ﷺ thus left for Madinah Munawwarah, and consummated the marriage at a place called Sarîf. Here too, Nabî ﷺ did not wait to emerge from ihram, before getting married. The nikâh took place immediately.

C) Nabî ﷺ did not wait for any special guests to arrive, nor did he make unnecessary efforts to call family members from far and wide, even though his ﷺ family (Qureish) were a very huge and respectable family. The sahâbah ؓ understood this temperament of Nabî ﷺ. It is for this reason that Hadrat Abdur Rahmân ibn Awf ؓ did not even inform Nabî ﷺ that he was getting married. When Nabî ﷺ saw a trace of yellow perfume on his clothing which was used on marriage occasions, Nabî ﷺ asked him what it was. Only then did he inform Nabî ﷺ that he had recently married. Nabî ﷺ did not become displeased why he was not invited, and not informed. We learn from this incident that the sahâbah were trained by Nabî ﷺ in such a way that they did not want to give him the difficulty of attending such functions. Furthermore, they did not feel it necessary to even inform him.

In this age, we find that people travel long distances wasting abundance of money to attend wedding functions. At times, ustâds (teachers) leave the great noble work of serving dîn and students shirk their lessons to be present. This is definitely exceeding the boundary of the shariah. In Islâhur-Rusûm, Hadrat Thânwi has stated, "There is no harm in inviting close relatives and friends on condition that the boundaries of the shariah are not compromised. The few nearby relatives should get together on the scheduled time without making unnecessary expenditure." The only reason people generally attend is to show face. They fear the insults and taunts of their family members. The money wasted on the travelling costs, clothing, etc. could rather be saved up and given to the bride and bridegroom discreetly, which could be then used to buy necessities in the home, which the newly-wed couple will always appreciate. However today, no thought is given to ikhlâs (doing actions for Allâh's pleasure) and granting benefit of others. Custom has become so ingrained in people that the right seems wrong, and the wrong appears to be right.

D) In all the nikâhs of Nabî ﷺ and the sahâbah ؓ, we find that there was no meal offered by the girl's party. The wedding feast which is all too common today, is not part of an Islamic wedding. Today unfortunately, more emphasis is given to this aspect than even the walîmah, which is undoubtedly sunnah. This custom has no Islamic origin. Most likely it stems from

Hindu or Christian custom, where the girl's party feeds the boy's party.

E.) The outstanding feature in all these marriages was simplicity. Nabî ﷺ said, "Simplicity is part of îmân." (Abu Dâwud, Ibn Majah) Moulânâ Muhammad Yusuf Saheb (rahimahullah) said, "The foundation of the social life of Rasulullâh ﷺ is based on purity, simplicity and modesty. The social life of the Jews is based on immodesty, extravagance and luxury." There were no honeymoons, preparations from months before, wastage in cards, halls, etc. For this reason, so much of goodness ensued from these marriages.

THE WALÎMAH

The hosting of walîmah is a sunnah of Nabî ﷺ as well as past messengers. The outstanding feature of these walimahs was simplicity. Whatever was easily and readily available would be served. According to majority of scholars, walimah is sunnah after cohabitation or at least some time spent in privacy. Some are of the view that walimah can take place after the nikâh is performed. This is referred to as *malâk* (see no. 3 below).

The actual object of walimah is to make apparent a halal and permissible connection. The best time to perform the walimah is the day after one has spent time with his spouse. Permission is also given for the second and third day.

If for some reason, the walimah could not be done at that time, then there is no harm if done later.

Walimah will remain a sunnah when these conditions are found:

1) The poor are invited – Rasulullâh ﷺ said, "The worst of food is the food of walimah in which the rich are invited and the poor are left out." (Bukhari, Muslim)
2) The walimah is done according to one's ability.
3) No interest-bearing loans are taken, since this person has been cursed by Nabî ﷺ, and by doing so is kept far away from the mercy of Allâh ﷻ.
4) There is no show and desire for praises and fame. Nabi ﷺ prohibited one from eating the food of those who are feeding for show and rivalry. (Abu Dâwud)
5) There is no formalities and unnecessary wastage and expenditure.
6) The walimah is done for Allâh ﷻ's pleasure, to follow the sunnah of Rasulullâh ﷺ. The clear sign of this is that one will abstain from all sins and not do such actions which cause the anger and displeasure of Allâh ﷻ and Rasulullâh ﷺ like music, intermingling of sexes, etc.

Hereunder are a few walimahs which took place in the time of Nabî ﷺ:

1) For the walimah of Hadhrat Fâtima ؓ, Hadhrat Sa'd ؓ offered a sheep he owned (for the meat) and the Ansaar collected a few *Saa* of wheat (for the bread).(Tabrâni)

2) The marriage of Hadrat Aa'isha ؓ was consummated in her parent's house. Neither was any camel nor any goat slaughtered

for her marriage until Sa'd bin Ubaadah sent a platter of food which he usually sent to Rasulullâh ﷺ whenever he was with any of his wives.(Ahmad)

3) After Najâshi had performed the marriage of Nabî ﷺ to Hadrat Umme Habîba, the Muslims started to leave. Najâshi ؓ said to them, "Do remain seated. It has been the practice of the Ambiyâ ؑ to host a meal on the occasion of a marriage. He then sent for the food and the Muslims ate before leaving." (Al-Bidâyah Wan Nihâyah)
If a meal is given on behalf of the man before the husband and wife meet, then this is referred to as malâk, and after meeting the meal is referred to as walimah.

4) After Rasulullâh ﷺ consummated his marriage with Hadrat Safiyya, Rasulullâh ﷺ had some *Hais* (a sweet dish made with dates, butter and flour) prepared and served on a leather tablecloth. Hadhrat Anas ؓ was then instructed to invite whoever was in the area (to partake of the food).

In another narration, Hadhrat Anas ؓ states that he invited the Muslims present there to a *Waleemah* meal that featured neither bread nor meat. All that it consisted of was Rasulullâh ﷺ's instruction to Bilaal ؓ to spread out a leather tablecloth. He then scattered some dates, cheese and butter onto it (which the people ate). (Bukhâri)

Hadhrat Jaabir ؓ reports, "When we gathered at the time of Isha, Rasulullâh ﷺ came out to us carrying in the edge of his shawl close to one and a half *Mudd* of Ajwah dates. (Handing them over to us) Rasulullâh ﷺ said, 'Eat from the *Waleemah* of your mother.'" (Ahmad)

5) Nabi ﷺ had a walimah after consummating his marriage to Zainab bint Jahsh ﺭ. He ﷺ fed the people to their fill with bread and meat. (Bukhâri) Another narration states, "Nabi ﷺ did not have a walimah as he had done for Zainab ﺭ. He made walimah with a sheep. (Bukhari, Muslim) The reason for extra care in this walimah was because this nikâh was performed in the heavens by Allâh ﷻ. People would arrive, eat and then leave. Then others would enter and do likewise. There were no formalities in hiring halls, etc. Whatever was easily available was utilized according to means.

6) Rabee'ah Aslami ﺭ hosted a walimah in which a sheep was slaughtered and bread was given.

CUSTOMS

Hadhrat Urwa bin Ruwaym reports that Hadhrat Abdullaah bin Qurt Thumaali ﺭ who was a companion of Rasulullâh ﷺ was appointed governor by Hadhrat Umar ﺭ. He was patrolling the streets of Hims one night when he passed by a bride in front of whom people were lighting several fires. Hadhrat Abdullaah ﺭ started hitting the people with his whip until they all dispersed. The next morning he sat on his pulpit and after duly praising Allâh ﷻ, he said, "When Abu Jandalah ﺭ married Umaamah ﺭ, he prepared some handfuls of food (as a *Waleemah*) for (his marriage to) her. May Allaah shower His compassion on Abu Jandalah ﺭ and may He shower His special mercies on

Umaamah ﷺ. May Allaah however curse your wedding of last night! The people were lighting fires and imitating the Kuffaar whereas Allaah has extinguished their light!"(Isâbah)

Allâh ﷻ states in Surah Hud, "And do not incline slightly to those who oppress, otherwise the Fire will touch you." It has been mentioned by reliable commentators of the Holy Quran that those who follow and imitate the nonbelievers and transgressors in personal looks, fashion and ways of living will fall within the ambit of the warnings mentioned in the abovementioned verse.(Ma'âriful Qurân)

Rasulullâh ﷺ said, "Whoever imitates a nation, will be regarded as one of them." (Abû Dâwûd) Under the explanation of the abovementioned Hadith, it has been mentioned that whosoever imitates or replicates the clothing, etc. of the non-Mulims, or those Muslims who transgress the rules of Shari'ah, will also have a share in their sins. Similarly, whosoever imitates the pious from amongst the believers, will have a share in the rewards of those pious people. (Bazlul-Majhûd)

Abdullâh ibn Abbâss ﷺ states that Nabî ﷺ said, "Three men incur the wrath of Allâh ﷻ." Amongst them is a person who adopts the rites and practises of the pagans.(Bukhârî)

Rasulullâh ﷺ said, "Whoever loves my sunnah, loves me, and whoever loves me, will be with me in Jannah."(Tirmidhi)

When it is said to them, "Follow what Allâh ﷻ has revealed," they say, "Nay! We shall follow the ways of our fathers. What! Even though their fathers were void of wisdom and guidance." (Baqarah 170)

In the book, *az-Zawâjir 'an Iqtirâf al-Kabâ'ir*, 'Allâmah Ibn Hajar Makkî Haythamî (rahimahullah) quotes a hadîth from Mâlik ibn Dînâr (rahimahullah) with regard to a revelation which Allâh ﷻ sent to a certain messenger saying:

> "Say to your people that they should not enter the entrances of My enemies, they should not wear the dress of My enemies, they should not ride the animals that are ridden by My enemies, and that they should not eat the food of my enemies. If not, they will become My enemies just as those are My enemies." *(Zawâjir)*

The harms of following customs are:

1.) The object is to please people. The ultimate objective of our lives in this world is to please Allah ﷻ; hence, any action done to solely please the creation of Allah ﷻ is disliked in Shari'ah. Consider the following. Rasulullâh ﷺ said, "Whoever does actions so that people can hear of it, Allâh ﷻ will make apparent to the creation his lowliness and despicability." (Bayhaqi in Shuabul-Imân)

Mulla 'Ali Qari (Rahimahullah) explains the meaning of the abovementioned Hadith that if a person does actions to show and please other people, Allah Ta'ala will make his bad habits known to everyone, and will ridicule him in this world.

Moreover, Nabi (Sallallahu Alaihi Wasallam) resembles such actions to ascribing partners to Allah Ta'ala and regards them as *Shirk Khafi* (a lower form of ascribing partners to Allah Ta'ala).

Shaddad bin Aus ﷺ was weeping one day. Thus, someone asked him as to why he was weeping. Upon this, he remarked that it is something I heard Nabi ﷺ saying; the memory of which makes me weep. He mentioned that he heard Nabi ﷺ saying, "I fear upon my ummah the lighter form of *shirk* and desire'. He says that upon this I asked Rasulullah ﷺ, "Will your ummah ascribe partners to Allah ﷻ after you?" Nabi ﷺ replied, "Yes; they will not worship the sun or the moon or stones or idols, but they will do actions to please others. (Bayhaqi in Shuabul-Imân)

2.) At times, people eventually begin to regard these customs as part of Islam, or they regard what is not obligatory as obligatory. If a person carries out an action thinking that it is part of Islâm, whilst it is not part of it, he will be sinful for his actions, as he has included in Islam what is not part of it. Nabi ﷺ said, "Whosoever innovates in Islam that which is not part of it, such an action is rejected and futile." (Bukhârî)

Hence, all practices in marriages that people regard as compulsory or give it the importance of a compulsory act of Shari'ah, will be considered impermissible in Shari'ah.

CHRISTIAN CUSTOMS:

1.) **Engagement rings and engagements** - The formal engagement ring began in the Roman era. The ring and solemn embrace gave the act mystic significance. Later on the tradition was carried on by the Christians. The significance of an engagement and the ring is a tradition based on the Christian ethos, western culture and superstition. Engagement is a mere promise to marry. In Islam there is no basis for the concept of an engagement party, and the sunnah is to marry the couple without unnecessary delay, once they have agreed to marry. Thus the engagement contract or party and the engagement rings are innovations introduced into Islam.

Gifts are received by the girl's party from the boy. If the girl's party demands such gifts, it will be regarded as bribery. Even if they do not demand the gifts, but it is a part of the custom to receive such gifts, the same ruling will apply. However, if no such custom prevails, then it will not be regarded as bribery.

2.) **Wedding ring** – Pope Nicholas 1 (c 866 CE) states that the whole Christian matrimony falls into two clearly defined parts: a) the preliminary betrothal i.e. the expression of consent by the parties and b) the delivery of the pledges, represented by the giving of the ring. The wedding ring has customarily symbolised an everlasting promise. Today dates and initials are engraved within it. The tradition for this dates back a long time. The ancient Greeks, the Jews and the Crusaders would engrave their rings with different messages. The importance of rings in a Christian wedding cannot be over-emphasised. The 'great authority' Charlemagne even declared that without the blessing of a marriage by a priest through rings, marriages should not be held valid. The wedding ring is placed on the forth finger. The English Christian custom dictates that, after the priest has blessed the ring, the bridegroom should place it, first, on the bride's thumb with the words "In the name of the Father" then on the index finger "and of the son" then on the middle finger "and of the holy ghost" and finally on the fourth finger "Amen."

3.) **The wedding dress or veil** – Traditionally, brides have been thought to be particularly vulnerable to evil spirits. The veils originally worn by Roman brides. It was thought that it would disguise the bride and therefore outwit any evil spirits. The veil became popular in Britain in the eighteen hundreds.

Fashion and the aristocracy introduced the white wedding dress. The first all-white wedding dress of modern times appears to have been worn by Ann of Brittany for her marriage to Louis X11. The word 'white wedding' have become neatly expressive of all the old traditions of white satin, bridesmaids, flowers, bells and wedding cakes. White epitomises purity and also is said to deter the evil eye.

4.) **Wearing of the crown (tiara)** – This is derived from early Christian tradition. Crowning typifies purity and at early Christian weddings the couple were crowned by the priest with garlands of myrtle (evergreen shrubs) after he had blessed the marriage ceremony. The importance of wearing a crown is held in such high esteem within the church that in some regions the crowns were bought by the parish and lent to all so that brides rich and poor might appear at their best on their wedding day. Even today, the Greek and Russian Christian marriages need two distinct ceremonies 1) the exchange of rings 2) crowning, a lengthy service where both parties express their consent to the union and towards the end the 'blessed' crown is placed on the head of the bride by the priest.

5.) **Wedding cake** – This is actually a symbol, whose origins are traced within the Christian Church. Previously bread would often be blessed at the end of the Sunday mass and distributed.

6.) **Flowers** – Using white or red flowers is amongst Christian culture. Western tradition would lead us to believe that flowers express fertility, love, and affection. It is important to note that Islam is not against flowers or their decorative use. The question raised here is the use of flowers on a special occasion in a ritualistic manner made obligatory by western Christian culture.

7.) **The best man** – It was the best man's duty to protect the groom from bad luck. He must ensure that once the groom has begun his journey to the church, he does not return for any reason. He must also arrange for the groom to carry a small mascot or charm in his pocket on the wedding day. When the best man is paying the church minister's fees, he should pay him an odd sum to bring luck to the couple.

HINDU CUSTOMS

Since many Muslims in South Africa and other countries hail originally from the Indo-Pak sub-continent, they have incorporated many Hindu customs in their marriages, which their forefathers practised there. A study of the rites of a Hindu marriage reveals that they are based on Vedic models laid down in Sanskrit in the Hindu laws. The marriage ritual has evolved into a complex, elaborate and expensive ceremony propagated by priests. The consideration of whom to invite, what presents to give and what to expect from others in future dealings seem prominent in a Hindu wedding.

1.) **Jann (or bârât)** – The Vivaha, a book for Hindus on marriage customs, spells out that on the wedding day, the groom with his friends and relatives goes to the house of the bride on a conveyance suited to his status (Jann party). In the past, elephants were recommended for the elite, nowadays they are replaced by expensive cars, horse and carriage, and in some cases, even helicopters. This is nothing but extravagance and show.

2.) **Mo'harue** – One elaborate ritual in Hindu marriages is the exchange of gifts. For this rite, a special occasion called Mo'harue is set aside. Special close relatives begin the process of giving presents followed by other invited guests. The object of this whole exercise is nothing but show. Islam encourages the exchanging of gifts, the objective being to solidify ties, and for mutual benefit and appreciation. In today's weddings, a great show is made by the giver, up to the point that presents are wrapped in transparent paper and exhibited to all before giving. The recipient makes a note in his diary of what he received and from whom, so that on future occasion, he knows what to give. There is no wholehearted exchange. The occasion is rather subject to what one has received in the past or what one expects in the future. There is no barakah (blessings), as the receiver considers it a burden as he will have to reciprocate with a similar gift in future, and the giver will silently suffer until he receives a similar gift.

In some communities there prevails a culture where the presents of the bride are kept by her parents. This is justified by them on the grounds that the bride has received them because the parents had given them in the past. This is completely incorrect.

3.) **Mehendi Ceremony**: This ceremony is held 2 to 3 days before Nikah. The bride-to-be and close relatives apply mehendi upon their hands and legs. In most mehendi ceremonies, music is played in the background and dandiya raas, or some other form of dance is performed. The prohibition of these things has been explained above. Money is also spent in having grand feasts on this day, resulting in extravagance. Some cultures carry out Hindu customs on this day, wherein the boy's party come in a procession with lamps in their hands. This is mere imitation of disbelievers, which cannot be tolerated in Shari'ah. Moreover, a special cream (besides the mehendi that is applied on the hands and legs) is applied on the whole body of the girl. If this is done simply to beautify herself for her husband, it will be permissible and virtuous for her to do so. However, in some cases, applying of mehendi results in the negligence of salah, as the mehendi cannot be washed off until firm. If any salah is omitted or delayed from its preferable time due to the applying of mehendi, then such applying will not be permissible.

4.) **Dandiya Raas**: Dandiya Raas is a type of a dance wherein the dancers hold two sticks and energetically whirl and move their feet and arms in a complicated, choreographed manner to the tune of the music with various rhythms. Its impermissibility is obvious due to the involvement of music and the intermingling of sexes. Besides being affiliated with impermissible acts, the dance itself originates from the Hindu culture. Origins of Raas are traced back to the teachings of Hinduism, wherein they mention that their "Lord Krishna" used to perform Raas Lila. The sticks used in Dandiya Raas are said to represent the swords of Durga (one of the Hindu goddesses), and Dandiya Raas is performed by Hindus at Navaratri (Hindu festival) and in Durga's honour. Adopting practices that symbolise other religions and hold religious values could take one out of the fold of Islam. Hence, the severity of the matter cannot be ignored.

WESTERN, MODERN CUSTOMS

The media is unfortunately influencing us in every aspect of our life. So much of effort, hardship and expense is undertaken, so that one can look 'just like the picture of the couple' as depicted on TV or in some novel.

1) **Photography and videoing** – Rasulullâh ﷺ has stated, "Angels (of mercy) do not enter a house in which there is a dog or where there are pictures." (Bukhâri, Muslim) When these angels are kept away, how can one expect blessings to arise from such a marriage which is 'blessed' by shaytân? The other harm of this sin is that as long as the picture remains in

existence, the person will be under divine displeasure. Other sins come to an end on one's demise. However here, even after one has left this world, the harmful effects of the photos and films will continue to afflict one. In another hadith, Nabî ﷺ said, "Those who will be the most severely punished on the Day of Judgement will be the picture-makers." (Bukhâri, Muslim) Nabi ﷺ has also mentioned, "Those people who make pictures will be given punishment on the Day of Judgement." It will be said to them, "Infuse life into that which you made." (Bukhâri, Muslim)

Special photographers are called on the day of nikah and walimah to video the whole ceremony and take pictures of the bride and the whole family. The male photographer is allowed to enter in the midst of all women and is also ordered to take pictures of the bride in different postures. Some have realised the harms of calling photographers, but photography still prevails through the medium of personal cameras and phones with cameras. They are only hiding their sins from people by not calling photographers, but they do not realise that Allah ﷻ is watching them violating His commandments. Moreover, the evil does not stop here, but CDs and albums of these pictures and videos are made, and those relatives who are non-mahram (with whom nikah is permissible) are given copies of these CDs. In some occasions videos and pictures of ladies functions are taken, wherein ladies who exercise strict hijâb are present. Their pictures are taken without their knowledge and viewed by non-mahrams with whom they were exercising strict hijâb. The act that is even more shameful is that parents show these videos and pictures to their young sons for them to choose their future wife. Even if these acts were not prohibited in Shari'ah, the modesty and bashfulness of a person with moderate thinking should stop him from such actions.

2) **Music and dancing** – Nabî ﷺ said, "Music creates hypocrisy in the heart just as water gives rise to crops." (Mishkât)

Hadhrat Anas Ibne Mâlik ﷺ stated, "That person who sits to listen to the singing of an immoral woman, then Allâh ﷻ will pour molten lead into his ears on the Day of Judgement." (Ibn Asâkir in his târîkh and Ibne-Sasri in his Amâli)

Nabi ﷺ said, "When my ummah become involved in 15 actions, then difficulties and trials will afflict them. When (1) booty will become a means of gathering money (2) trust will be regarded as booty (3) zakât will become a burden (4,5,6,7) men will follow their wives, disobey their mothers, be kind to their friends, and harsh to their fathers (8) voices will be raised in the masâjid (9) the worst of people will be leaders (10) the leader will become the lowest and most despised (11) people will be honoured due to fear (12) alcohol will be drunk (13) silk will be worn (14) singing women and musical instruments will become common (15) the last people of this ummah will curse the people of past generations; at such a time, wait for red storms, sinking in the earth and the disfiguration of faces." (Tirmidhi)

Hadhrat Abû Hurayrah ﷺ stated that Nabi ﷺ said, "In the last era, from my ummah, the faces of one group will be transformed into that of dogs and pigs."

The Sahâbah ﷺ said, "O messenger of Allâh, will these people be Muslims?" Nabi ﷺ replied, "Yes, they will bear witness of لا اله الا الله محمد رسول الله and they will fast."

The Sahâbah ﷺ asked, "Why will this happen to them?"

Nabi ﷺ answered, "They will be involved in the usage of musical instruments, have singing girls and will began using the drum. They will be involved in taking alcohol. One night they will be intoxicated in alcohol and merry-making, and the next morning their figure will be transformed." (Ibn Hibbân)

Nabî ﷺ said that he had been sent to destroy musical instruments. (Abu Dâwud)

Besides this, there are many ahâdîth which show the prohibition of such songs which are immoral, futile and which incite the passions.

OTHER EVILS

1) **Wedding feast** - The time of marriage is a time of sorrow for the girl's family and the girl as well as a time of happiness. Out of happiness for this bounty, the husband invites people for the walimah. Even though logically the woman is happy, her shame, sorrow and modesty demands that she does not exhibit this happiness. Together with this, there is no precedent for this feast in the lives of the Sahâbah or the pious predecessors.

Since this feast is given more importance than even the walimah and is regarded as binding, it should be completely abandoned.

If the boy is from a distant place and nikâh is performed at such a time when meals are generally served, there is no harm in partaking of this meal as this is given on the basis of hospitality. However, having a special meal, inviting huge numbers of people, hiring of halls, printing of wedding cards, sitting on stages, etc. is against the way of Islamic culture.

2.) Missing of salâh – The greatest act of worship in Islâm is that of salâh. During marriages, salâh is abandoned completely. Even those who are in the habit of performing salâh generally, more-so amongst the women-folk, neglect their salâh or perform it as qadhâ. When this is our condition with the most important of Allâh ﷻ's laws, then how can we expect to draw Allâh ﷻ's mercy and benevolence at such an occasion? The bride at times wears such types of outfits, wherein it is not possible for her to perform salâh. Most of the ceremonies last till late at night, resulting in the forfeiting of Fajr salâh. The people of the house are so engrossed in the preparations for all these ceremonies and entertaining their guests that they tend to forget salâh, or delay it from its mustahab time. Resulting in negligence of salâh itself is enough to render these ceremonies impermissible.

3) Extravagance and Wastage – Allâh ﷻ states, "Eat and drink, and do not waste. Verily Allâh ﷻ does not love those who waste." In another verse, Allâh ﷻ states, "And grant family members their right, the poor and the travellers; and do not waste. Verily those who waste are the brothers of Shaytân. Shaytân was ungrateful to his creator." As mentioned earlier, the marriage with the least expense leads to the greatest amount of blessings.

Therefore, all unnecessary expenses in a marriage will be regarded as extravagance and will fall under the prohibition mentioned above.
A few examples of extravagance and wastage are:

a.) **Wedding cards**: Thousands are spent in the printing of wedding cards with the latest designs and best quality. This will be considered extravagance and will not be permissible according to Shari'ah. If there is a real need to print wedding cards so as to inform people of the wedding, it will be permissible to do so, on condition that the wedding cards are simple and moderate. However, it has been noticed that many a time a guest is invited personally or over the phone and thereafter a card is also sent to him. This will not be regarded as permissible as it is apparent that there was no need for the card.

b.) **Grand wedding halls**: Grand halls are booked for the day of the Nikah and *walimah* and thousands are spent in the decoration of such halls. This will also fall under extravagance. Some go to the extent of booking halls in luxury hotels that sell alcohol and pork in them. There is a fear of contamination of the liquor and pork in the food served; hence, Islam commands us to stay away from such places.

c.) **Luxury cars**: Using of luxury cars for the bride and the groom is also found in the practice of many Muslims. The main object behind using these cars is to show other people, which is prohibited. Money is also wasted in decorating the car, which is extravagance. Moreover, this practice stems from the Hindu culture wherein the bridegroom used to ride on a horse or elephant to the wedding ceremony. The Hindus then started replacing it with luxury cars. Hence, such practice will be regarded as imitating the disbelievers.

d.) **Travelling overseas for wedding shopping**: It has become a trend in many cultures to travel overseas to purchase goods for the wedding. A feeble excuse is made that the latest fashion in clothing is not available in the country. In the process, thousands of dollars are spent for plane tickets, accommodation, etc.

e.) **Lighting up the house**: Many parents take pleasure in decorating and lighting the house with colorful bulbs. This is a waste of money and electricity. There is no doubt in regarding this as extravagance, as there is no real need for this lighting as is done only to show other people, which is also prohibited.

f.) **Ceremonies before and after marriage**: The ceremonies of marriage start a week or two before marriage, and close relatives are invited every day to these ceremonies. Ceremonies are also held a few days after the *walimah*, wherein the groom and close relatives are invited by the bride's parents. A ceremony is also held on the day of Nikah. Special menus are prepared for each day, and large sums of money are spent in these feasts. Moreover, although entertaining guests itself is something encouraged in Shari'ah, these ceremonies are regarded as compulsory and held merely to please other people, the prohibitions of which have been elaborated above.

Even worse today is the stag parties held which is totally shameless and a satanic innovation.

Hadrat Thanwi said, "A person complained to me, 'At times of happiness, I would like to spend a huge sum of money. When Allâh ﷻ has given me money, why should I not spend? You prevent us from spending in many avenues, show us one avenue in which we can spend." I said to him, "If you wish to spend, then the way of doing this, according to intellect, is to prepare a list of poor people. Whatever amount you wish to spend, distribute it amongst them (spend that amount in the marriages of poor households). See how much of fame you will get, even though this should not be your intention. (In this case,) so much of benefit will be granted to the poor. If you want to spend the money on your family, then the best way is to do what a rich person did when his daughter got married (instead of wasting his money on foolish customs), he bought a property of one hundred thousand rupees for his daughter. He said, "My intention was to spend one hundred thousand rupees. For this reason, I had kept this amount aside. Then I thought that what benefit will my daughter (and son-in-law) receive with all this clamour and hue? People will eat and depart, money will be wasted, and my daughter will gain no benefit. I therefore adopted this manner through which my daughter will benefit. There is nothing better than property. For generations, my daughter and her progeny will benefit from its profits. No-one can now call me stingy, because even though I did not use my money for all these futilities, I did not keep the money in my house." This is the way of intelligent people."

The main object of fulfilling these customs is for show and fame. A person desires that he must be remembered and praised for his function. Remember that in most cases, after the function, there are thousands of complaints. Very few people are satisfied. No matter how many people are invited, there will be so many who will be upset due to not being invited. Then the people generally invited are from the wealthier class. The food will never be up to their standard. If a person achieves a bit of fame for a few days, then as soon as a new custom emerges, people say, "What did he do? Look how the other surpassed him!" When problems afflict one, then none of those for whom you spent so much will stand at your side. In fact, they will pass remarks, "Who told him to waste money? He destroyed himself."

Hadrat Thanwi said, "We have seen people who when in good conditions, people said to them, "Where your perspiration falls, we are prepared to sacrifice our blood." However, when difficulties afflicted that person, not even one person stood by him. All closed their eyes, and changed their attitude completely." This is the condition of man who is most unfaithful. If on the other hand, one pleases Allâh ﷻ, he will never be at loss, since Allâh ﷻ is the most faithful. He ﷻ will never leave one in the lurch. Another great problem which arises due to these functions is jealousy. Outwardly people appear to be well-wishers, but many have hearts of wolves. They will search for faults in the function, so that the host can be disgraced and embarrassed.

Many times, loans are procured for fulfilling these customs. This exacerbates the sin. People have destroyed their live-savings in trying to fulfil these traditions. Never mind wasting the money, it is not even permissible for one to advance a loan to some-one for fulfilment of these customs, since one will be a cause for this sin.

3) **Intermingling of sexes** – The prohibition of intermingling of sexes is not something alien to Muslims. However, due to affiliation with other religions and sects, they fail to understand that close relatives like cousins and sisters-in-law are also non-mahram, and hijâb is obligatory with them too; and they freely mix with these relatives, especially in the ceremonies before Nikah. They make simple excuses like we grew up together, without taking into consideration that they are openly violating a command of Allah ﷻ mentioned in the Holy Quran. The consequences of such violation of the commandments of Allah can be very detrimental, and could lead to kufr (disbelief) in cases where a person clearly refuses to accept such a law and regards it permissible.

4) **Taking of loans** – It is prohibited to take loans for the performance of marriages, just to fulfil customs, and wherein there is wastage.
Moderation in spending is the instruction of Islâm. If people are moderate in expenditure and abstain from extravagance, they

will never be dependent on others. Overspending and failing to budget one's income lead to debt which in turn brings disgrace, worry and frustration. People are financially ruined, and, along with such worldly ruin, comes spiritual ruin as well.

Among the worst of calamities is debt, especially if one has no means of paying the debts. Rasulullâh ﷺ has sounded dire warnings in regard to unpaid debt. Nabî ﷺ said that whoever incurs a debt and has no intention of repaying it, will pay with his good deeds for it on the Day of Judgement. If his good deeds are not sufficient, the sins of the creditor will be recorded in his name. (Bayhaqî) Even martyrdom is no absolution for debt. A martyr will be forgiven all his sins, but debt. Debt will be demanded even in the hereafter.

1) In this regard, Rasulullâh ﷺ said, "I take an oath by that Being in whose possession is my life that the man who is in debt will not enter Jannah even if he is martyred; then he is resurrected and again martyred; then again is resurrected and again martyred. He will not enter Jannah until his debt is paid." (Nasâi, Hâkim)

2) Once a bier was brought before Rasulullâh ﷺ so that he could perform the janâzah salâh. Nabî ﷺ asked, "Does he have any debts?" When the Sahâbah ؓ replied in the affirmative, Nabî ﷺ remarked, "Jibraîl ؈ prohibited me from performing salâh on one who has debts. The debtor is held back in the grave (from the bounties of Jannah) until his debts are absolved." (Abû Ya'lâ) Another narration states, "The sahâbah ؓ were in the presence of Nabî ﷺ. A bier was brought so that

Nabî ﷺ could perform salâh over it. Nabî ﷺ asked, "Does your companion have any debts?" When the sahâbah ؓ replied in the affirmative, Nabî ﷺ said, "What benefit will you derive if I perform salâh on a man whose soul is detained in his grave and cannot rise to the heavens. If some-one takes responsibility for his debts, I will stand and perform salâh over him, then my salâh will benefit him." (Tabrâni)

3) Abû Saîd ؓ narrates that he heard Rasulullâh ﷺ saying: "I seek refuge in Allah from *kufr* and debts." A person asked: "O Rasulullâh! Do you regard *kufr* and debts to be equal that you are mentioning them together?" He replied, "Yes." (Nasâî)

4) Rasulullâh ﷺ said, "Debts is the flag of Allah on earth. When He wishes to disgrace anyone, He burdens him with the weight of debts." (Hâkim)

5) Rasulullâh ﷺ advised a person in the following manner, "Reduce your sins so that your death will be easy. Reduce your debts so that you may live a free person." (Bayhaqî)

6) Rasulullâh ﷺ said, "The person who marries a woman with *mahr*, whether it be a small amount or a large amount, and has this intention that he will not pay her the *mahr* and passes away without paying her, then on the day of judgement he will rise as an adulterer in the presence of Allah. And the person who takes a loan with the intention of not paying it back and passes away without fulfilling it, will rise as a thief in the presence of Allah on the day of judgement." (Tabrânî in Saghîr and Awsat)

5) **Beauty parlours** – Visiting of beauty parlours during the marriage ceremonies has also become a trend. The bride and close relatives spend hours in the beauty parlour to get their hair done and face made up according to the fashion set by the disbelievers. This will fall under the ruling of imitating the disbelievers. In the process, salâhs are omitted and a lot of money is spent. Moreover, most of the make-up used do not comply with the standards of Shari'ah, thus, could result in the invalidity of *salah* performed in them. We should also remember that it is not permissible for a Muslim woman to expose any portion of her body besides her face and hands in front of a non-Muslim woman. In front of other Muslim women, the area between the navel and knee cannot be exposed. Cutting and trimming of one's hair is not permitted.

6) **Clothing** – Nabi ﷺ said, "Whoever wears clothing for show, Allâh Ta'âlâ will make him wear the clothing of disgrace on the Day of Judgement." (Ahmad, Abû Dâwud, Nasaî)

"Clothing for show" means that a person wears beautiful and expensive clothing to make apparent his greatness and so that he can boast. This show will create pride and arrogance. Allâh ﷻ despises a proud person.

Many Muslims adopt dressing that resemble with the dressing of the actors and actresses of Bollywood. Dresses worn by certain actors in certain films are ordered or custom made. This clearly falls under the rule of imitating the disbelievers and transgressors. Would we prefer to be resurrected amongst these actors and actresses on the day of Qiyamah? This is a very severe matter to which people do not pay much heed. Moreover, money is wasted in buying the branded and extravagant clothing and some even travel overseas to purchase clothing to keep up with the fashion, mention of which has already been made. The most money is spent on the bride's dress for the Nikah and the walimah ceremonies. Today, thousands, if not hundreds of thousands, are spent in procuring clothing for wedding functions, which, in most cases are generally never worn again.

'Abdul Wahid bin Aiman narrates from his father who says that one day he went to 'Aishah ☪ and she was wearing a coarse dress costing five Dirhams. 'Aishah ☪ said, "Look at my slave-girl who refuses to wear it in the house. I had a similar dress during the lifetime of Nabi ﷺ. Every woman in Madinah desiring to appear elegant (before her husband) borrowed it from me." (Bukhârî) This hadith portrays the simplicity of the women of Madina in the time of Nabi ﷺ. They did not waste money in buying a dress to adorn themselves in front of their husbands, which is in fact permissible in Shari'ah.

7.) **The exchanging of gifts and trousseau**: The exchanging of gifts in itself is an act of virtue and encouraged in Shari'ah. However, it is an undeniable fact that the two parties are compelled to give out these gifts. The relatives to whom gifts have to be given out are stipulated through custom; for example, a certain amount is stipulated for the mother-in-law, a certain amount for sister-in-law, etc. This is clear proof that these gifts are given through compulsion and not with the intention of giving gifts as such; hence, will not be permissible.

The same applies to the giving out of trousseau. There is no harm in a father giving out whatever he wishes to his daughter, as long as he is giving it from his own free will. However, in many cases the boy's party demands the trousseau; and even in the cases trousseau is not demanded, the custom prevails that trousseau has to be given and it is understood between the parties that the trousseau will be given by the girl's father. Some of them who are poor have to borrow money or take zakat in order to give a trousseau. This is proof of compulsion of something not obligatory, which is prohibited in Shari'ah. Moreover, the giving out of trousseau has taken the form of competition, wherein one Muslim tries to excel his fellow Muslim brother in buying a better trousseau than the other. Some go to the extent of travelling overseas to buy the dowry. This undoubtedly will fall under extravagance. The ones who cannot afford do not wish to be left out, and spend over and above their means in keeping up with the competition. This results in people borrowing money from others, or taking zakat in order to have a marriage that would please others. The question remains that in spite of all the above-mentioned, can we still regard the exchanging of gifts and the giving of trousseau as permissible?

Nowadays, bridal showers are held. The non-Muslims have coined a novel concept of begging – especially amongst the upper-class. In the name of Bridal Showers, people gracefully and politely extend their hands, and they ask and take from others.

The bride-to-be chooses her gifts from exclusive stores that offer a "registry" or she unashamedly hands out a list of those items she wants gifted to her. In the process, she places pressure and financial difficulty and sometimes a great burden on others - to purchase those gifts that she has chosen.

At the get-together, these gifts and other gifts are presented to the bride-to-be, who opens them and shows them to all present – and each person can assess the kind of money that was spent on the gift given. There are various wrongs in this act:

a.) A person is forced to purchase gifts that the bride has chosen – which may be beyond her budget in spending.
b.) A person who gives something simple or inexpensive will feel ashamed and embarrassed, considering the manner in which gifts are being received and shown to others.
c.) Gifts are not given happily. There is no blessings in such gifts.
Besides this, many immoral actions generally take place at such functions. It is not permissible to even go for these functions.

8.) **Ceremonies for showing gifts and trousseau**: In some cultures, special ceremonies are held to show the relatives what gifts were given out and what trousseau was given out. Announcements are made as to who is giving the gift to whom and the value of the gift. At times, the entire trousseau given out is displayed, and each and every person invited has a look at the trousseau. These are merely customs that are being followed for ages, and are against the teachings of Shari'ah as they are regarded compulsory. Moreover, the main objective of these ceremonies is to show off the goods to others.

9.) **Exorbitant dowries:** By fixing over-priced dowries, it becomes difficult for young women to get married. For this reason, Umar ؓ once stood on the pulpit and gave the following sermon, "Take note that you should not inflate the dowries of your women because had this been an act of honour in this world and an act of Taqwa in Allâh's sight, Nabî ﷺ would have been most entitled to it. However, Rasulullâh ﷺ never gave any of his wives a dowry of more than twelve *Awqiya* and did not receive more than this as dowry for any of his daughters either. What is happening is that some of you inflate the dowry so much that the husband (when unable to pay) fosters hatred for her in his heart, saying, 'It is because of you that I have been burdened with a water-bag hung around my neck.'' (Tirmidhi, Abu Dâwûd, Nasaî, Ibn Majah)

Hadhrat Masrooq narrates that Hadhrat Umar ؓ once mounted the pulpit and said, "O people! What is this inflation of dowries for your women when the dowries common amongst Rasulullâh ﷺ and his Sahâbah ؓ were in the region of four hundred Dirhams and less. Had inflated dowries been a sigh of Taqwa in Allaah's sight or a mark of honour, you people would have never beat Rasulullâh ﷺ and his Sahâbah ؓ to it (they would have been first to implement it)." (Abu Ya'al and Said ibn Mansûr)

10.) **Honeymoons:** It is an imitation of the non-Muslims and it is a great waste of money. It also leads to neglect of many religious matters, like salah, etc. Many sins are normally committed in resorts and hotels, etc. where people spend their first few days of their marriage life. It was the habit of the pious predecessors to spend the beginning of their married life in their own homes. The modern formula of the bride and groom leaving for a destination after the ceremony only really started in Victorian times in England.

ACTIONS AFTER MARRIAGE

(1.) The bridegroom should place his hand on the fore-head (by the forelocks) of the bride, take the name of Allâh ﷻ and make dûa of barakah (blessings) for the bride. Nabi ﷺ had said, "When any of you get married, then he should place his hands on the forehead, take the name of Allâh, and make duâ for goodness by saying,

اَللّٰهُمَّ إِنِّي اَسْئَلُكَ مِنْ خَيْرِهَا وَخَيْرِ مَا جَبَلْتَهَا عَلَيْهِ وَاَعُوْذُ بِكَ مِنْ شَرِّهَا وَشَرِّ مَا جَبَلْتَهَا عَلَيْهِ

"O Allâh! I ask you for her goodness and the goodness of that which You have placed in her. I seek Your protection from her harm and the harm of that which You have placed in her."
(Bukhâri, Abû Dâwûd)

(2.) The bride and bridegroom should perform some rakats of nafl (optional) salâh, and then make duâ of goodness and blessings. (Abu Nuaym in Hilyah)

(3.) The bridegroom should speak to his bride and should offer her something to eat or drink. When Nabi ﷺ went to Hadhrat Ayesha ؓ, he brought one container of milk. He drank from there and then gave her. She lowered her head due to shame and modesty. Without doubt, this is a beautiful way of removing her fear and a cause of strengthening the bond of love and affection between the two. A famous saying is that a kind of fear comes with every oncoming person, and fear overcomes every strange person.

(4.) An etiquette of sexual intercourse is that the male and female should not be completely naked. Nabi ﷺ has stated, "Verily Allâh Ta'âlâ is full of modesty and concealment, He loves modesty and concealment." (Ahmad, Tirmidhi)
Nabi ﷺ also said, "Beware of becoming naked, since there are with you those angels who do not separate from you except at the time of sexual relations and relieving oneself. Therefore, be modest in front of them and honour them." (Tirmidhi) This means that husband and wife should be covered by some sheet even though their clothing are removed.

(5.) Another etiquette is that the man should first kiss and fondle her. Nabi ﷺ said, "None of you should fall onto his wife like an animal. First there should be some messenger. "It was asked, "O Rasûl of Allâh (ﷺ), what is the messenger?" Nabi ﷺ replied, "Speaking and kissing." (Musnad Firdaws of Daylami) Based on this hadîth, Imâm Ghazâli رحمه الله تعالى writes in his book Ihyâul-ulûm that when the husband fulfils his desire, then he should grant her the opportunity to complete her enjoyment. At times, it takes woman time to ejaculate. Therefore, if he moves away immediately, it can become a cause of causing harm to her. It can even lead to disgust and hatred.

(6.) Before intercourse, this duâ should be recited

بِسْمِ اللهِ اَللّٰهُمَّ جَنِّبْنَا الشَّيْطٰنَ وَجَنِّبِ الشَّيْطَانَ مَا رَزَقْتَنَا

In the name of Allâh, O Allâh, protect us from shaytân and keep shaytân away from the children that you will grant us.
(Bukhâri)

If Allâh Ta'âlâ has decreed children due to this union, they will be saved from the influence of shaytân.

(7.) A man may have intercourse with his wife in any manner provided it is through the vagina. Allâh Ta'âlâ has mentioned,

نِسَاؤُكُمْ حَرْثٌ لَكُمْ فَأْتُوا حَرْثَكُمْ أَنَّى شِئْتُمْ

"Your wives are a tillage for you, thus go to your farms from wherever you want." (Baqarah)

This means that a person could have vaginal intercourse with his wife in whichever manner he wants, either from in front of her, behind her or lying on the side.

(8.) If after having intercourse once, there is a desire to have it a second time, then it is mustahab (commendable) to first make wudhu. This will increase pleasure and desire.

Nabi ﷺ has mentioned, "When any person has had intercourse with his wife, and desires to have a second time, then he should perform wudhu, because by making wudhu there is more pleasure." (Abû Dâwûd)

If between two sessions, ghusl (bath) is performed, then this is much better as is proven in a hadîth.

(9.) It is better for both to have ghusl as soon as possible. If due to tiredness, one cannot perform ghusl before sleeping, then it is mustahab (commendable) to at least perform wudhu before sleeping. This was the practice of Nabi ﷺ as narrated by Hadhrat Ayesha ﷺ. (Abû Dâwûd)

PROHIBITTED ACTIONS

(1.) It is completely forbidden for the husband or wife to discuss their private matters and sexual relations with anyone, in words or by indication.

Nabi ﷺ has said, "On the day of Judgment, the lowest person in status in the sight of Allâh Ta'âlâ will be a person who had sexual relations with his wife, and then mentioned those matters to others." (Muslim, Abû Dâwud)

(2.) It is harâm (unlawful) to have anal intercourse. Nabi ﷺ has stated, "Allâh Ta'âlâ will not glance with mercy at that person who has anal intercourse." (Nasaî, Ibn Hibbân)
Nabi ﷺ has also said, "Accursed is the person who has anal intercourse with his wife." (Abû Dâwud)
Together with anal intercourse being harmful from a medical point of view, it is also contrary to honour and noble character.

(3.) It is harâm (unlawful) to have sexual intercourse when one's wife is menstruating or during nifâs (bleeding after childbirth).
Allâh ﷻ has stated,

$$فَاعْتَزِلُوا النِّسَاءَ فِى الْمَحِيْضِ$$

"Stay away (from sexual intercourse) from women during their menses." (Baqarah)

Yes, in these conditions, the husband can fondle and take pleasure over a piece of cloth covering the portion between the navel and knees. However, it is not permissible to take any enjoyment under this piece of cloth, so that one does not fall into any prohibited and harmful action. The shepherd who grazes his sheep on the boundaries of someone else's field always fears that perhaps his sheep may enter that field.

Therefore, a Muslim should always remain cautious in matters of religion and health. He should always choose that path and way in all his matters, dealings and actions in which there is more precaution and in which lies greater piety.

A few other prohibited and disliked acts:
1.) Watching pornographic material for stimulation
2.) Fantasizing about another person during intercourse
3.) Oral sex
4.) Taking pictures and even worse, intimate pictures of one another
5.) Cross dressing
6.) Bondage and flogging
7.) Husband drinking wife's milk
8.) Using food during foreplay
9.) Using sex aids during foreplay
10.) Sexually provocative dancing accompanied by music

To live a happy married life, we should try to follow the following guidelines mentioned by our respected ulamâ. By doing so, Allâh ﷻ will grant a person the enjoyment of Jannah in this world.

ETIQUETTES OF SPOUSES

The family is the nucleus of an Islamic society and marriage is the only way to bring families into existence. A healthy Muslim society depends on a sound Islamic environment. Happy couples make happy families, who make healthy societies. The union of two souls is the fibre which weaves society together. For this reason, Nabi ﷺ emphasized the importance of appropriate conduct after marriage so that it endures and becomes the 'coolness of the eyes', in the words of the Qur'an. A happy marriage is not made in heaven, nor does it flourish on its own. It has to be continually nurtured and preserved. Marriage can be a source of enormous tranquillity, yet it can also become a root of the greatest pain, sorrow and heartbreaks. Once two people have committed themselves to each other they should move mountains in order to stay together. It takes time and effort to blend two lives. Many marriages do not last because partners take the view that if it does not work, they will simply end the marriage. This shows lack of commitment, a lack of drive and is deficient by nature. This marriage is almost doomed from the start.

Marriage is very similar to constructing a building. It requires a strong foundation that can withstand the storms and shocks of stress. The adhesive that binds couples together is love and mercy. By acting on the following guidelines, Insha-Allaah, our marriages will become more enjoyable, love will increase and we will attain success in both worlds.

1.) Always make duâ for one's spouse and for a happy marriage.
2.) Adopt taqwa (Allâh consciousness) and be mindful of your duties to Allâh ﷻ at all times, as piety is the stepping stone to a beautiful moral and spiritual character.
3.) Create an Islamic environment at home, as this will bring peace and serenity in your lives.
4.) Do not be concerned with fulfilling your own religious duties. It is your religious and moral obligation to encourage your spouse and children towards their Islamic duties with love, wisdom and patience.
5.) Acquaint yourself with the knowledge, reality and responsibilities of marriage. Remember that marriage is not only fulfilment of carnal desires but fulfilment of responsibilities.
6.) Under no circumstances should you compel your spouse or children to obey you in any act that contravenes the commands of Allâhﷻ. At the same time, you should not succumb to the un-Islamic dictates of your spouse and children.
7.) If any problem or dispute arises in the marriage, then always turn to Allâh ﷻ for help and guidance first. If the problem persists, consult a pious experienced elder or alim for advice.
8.) Live simply. Don't be jealous of those who seem to be living a more luxurious life than your family. Sustenance is from Allâh ﷻ. In order to inculcate contentment, look at those people who have less than you, not those who have more.
9.) Be mindful of your discussion topics. Never discuss things with others about your marriage that your spouse would not like to discuss, unless there is an Islamic reason to do so. Some husbands and wives, believe it or not, complain to others about

their spouse's physical appearance. This is a recipe for disaster. Information about your intimate relations should be kept between you and your spouse.
10.) As far as possible, try to have meals together as a family. Express your appreciation, whether the cook is the husband or wife. Rasulullâh ﷺ would not complain about food put in front of him. Do not look for faults.
11.) Exchange gifts. This creates love.

ETIQUETTES FOR HUSBANDS

Allâh ﷻ says, "For them (women) are rights similar to those on them according to the beautiful standard." Man is told that as there are rights due to him, his wife also has rights due unto her.
Rasulullâh ﷺ said, "The best among you are those who are best towards their wives." (Tirmidhi).

1.) When entering the home, always make salâm cheerfully, no matter how difficult your day may have been.
2.) Similarly, when leaving home in the morning, make a point of kissing your wife and don't leave without salaam. Salâm is a means of engendering great love and happiness in the home.
3.) Implement the beautiful sunnah of smiling. Smile more and frown less. Express this virtuous act of smiling to your wife often, and not only outside to strangers. Smiling is an act of charity. *Try and create such a loving presence at home that your family members look forward to see you, rather than hoping you never come home.*

4.) Support and spend generously on your family, <u>according to your means.</u> Regard this as an Islamic responsibility, not as a favour upon them, nor as a burden on you.

5.) Spending on bare necessities is not sufficient to engender true love and a happy home. However, be moderate in your expenditure- there should be neither wastage nor miserliness.

6.) Shower your wife with gifts (within means). Never remind her of favours you confer on her.

7.) Provide her with her own monthly allowance (according to means) over and above your house hold budget expenses. This money will then **belong to her,** thus allowing her freedom of choice to purchase items for her personal needs, without having to account how it was spent.

8.) Compliment your wife's cooking after meals. Overlook the little shortcomings, e.g. if the salt is less or if the food is not prepared on time, for some reason beyond her control.

9.) Endeavour to eat and drink from the same utensil. Sometimes place a morsel of food in each other's mouth (not only to be practised when newly-wed), this will increase mutual love. One will be rewarded for this.

10.) Do not disclose your wife's secrets or faults to either family members or friends. Always conceal one another's faults. Even worse is to speak about one's physical relationship.

11.) Express your love often and make her feel wanted. According to Rasulullâh ﷺ, the mercy of Allâh ﷻ pours on a couple when the husband glances at his wife with love and pleasure and she reciprocates by glancing at him with love and pleasure.

12.) Laugh and joke with her within Shar'i limits. Nabi ﷺ used to engage in light-hearted conversation with his wives.

13.) Compliment your wife on her dressing. If you do not approve of any aspect of her dressing, then instead of rebuking her, rather explain to her in a gentle and loving manner your likes and dislikes. *Just as you would like to see her smartly dressed, you too should dress smartly for her (all within the confines of the shari'ah).*

14.) If possible, give her a call during the day to see how she is feeling.

15.) Share in the upkeep and maintenance of the home. Doing household chores is a sunnah of Nabî ﷺ that breeds humility and displays compassion and kindness. Nabî ﷺ assisted in household chores. Examples of this are cleaning, sweeping, laying the food-cloth, looking after the children.

16.) Learn to tolerate slight misbehaviour, or displeasing little acts committed by your wife. Don't react violently by meting out injustice and cruelty upon her with verbal and physical abuse. Never take her curse. Don't break your promises, crush all expectations and become an oppressor, a tyrant and a blackmailer. Unfortunately, many of our sisters bear untold misery and suffer in silence, day in and day out for years on end, having none to turn to besides Allâh ﷻ. Remember O husband, when that lonely, broken heart cannot tolerate anymore and those hands rise up complaining to none other than Allâh ﷻ, then rest assured that her tears and pain will not go unanswered. Nabî ﷺ has stated, "Beware the curse of the oppressed person, since there is no veil between it and Allâh ﷻ." Allâh ﷻ says to the oppressed person, "I will assist you, even though it be after some time."

17.) Endeavour to change her habits like carelessness, laziness, etc. with advice and admonition. This must be given tactfully, with wisdom and patience. **Rule with love and never with the iron fist.** It is among her rights upon you that you tolerate her. Nabî ﷺ has said that a woman is created from a crooked rib and there is therefore crookedness in her character. If you try to straighten her, you will destroy her. Therefore, take benefit from her together with her crookedness.

18.) Live with her and speak in the manner that you would want someone to treat your own sister or daughter. If you dislike some qualities in them, they possess others pleasing to you. Look at these qualities. No one is perfect. Remember the grass always seems greener on the other side.

19.) When you are overcome by anger and wish to physically or verbally abuse her, then remember that Allâh ﷻ, whose trust she is, possesses greater power than you do. Immediately move away from that place, drink water and recite *ta'awudh* (i.e. audhu billâhi minash shaytân ir rajîm.) If possible, make wudhu. Remember that after the expression of every bout of anger, there is regret. Never discuss a problem in the state of anger. Calm down first.

20.) Learn to forgive your wife- Forgive her as many times as you would like Allâh ﷻ to forgive you for your errors. Remember the English adage "To err is human, to forgive is Divine."

21.) Regard your wife's parents as your own, address them politely and treat them kindly as you would treat your own parents. Accord them the same respect and honour as your own parents.

22.) Learn to communicate constructively. Make a resolution that at the time of a problem you would sit down and discuss in a dignified manner, without raising voices or being abusive; or you will seek advice from someone you both can confide in.

23.) You cannot choose not to communicate-even your silence and body language can send important messages. However, they may be misinterpreted and could cause more harm.

24.) Misunderstandings and minor differences should not be suppressed. Rather discuss them in an amicable manner; else this could ultimately lead to a broken marriage (Allâh ﷻ save us.)

25.) **Learn to admit your mistakes. This is a sign of humility. Do not attempt to justify your mistakes.**

26.) Don't ever argue in public or in front of the children. This can affect the children psychologically and could prove detrimental to the marriage.

27.) In a serious conflict, call in arbitrators from both sides and let the matter be solved amicably.

28.) **Spend quality time with your wife and children.** The time spent with them is an act of ibâdah (worship). Apart from religious activities and necessary business activities, devote yourself to your family. Insha-Allaah, it will reap excellent dividends.

29.) Control your tongue at all times. Remember that wounds afflicted by swords may heal, but the wounds afflicted by the tongue very seldom heal.

30.) Never compare nor mention the beauty, character or qualities of other women to your wife. This is extremely insensitive and may cause jealousy, suspicion and unnecessary doubts in her mind. Accept your wife for what she is and do not cast lustful glances at other women. By doing so, shaytân will beautify the form of these other women. When a woman emerges from her home, shaytân beautifies her in the eyes of men. By controlling one's gazes, one's love for his wife will increase and one will attain the sweetness of imân.

31.) Do not keep in touch or communicate with any female acquaintances from the past, even if they are 'just good friends'. This is extremely detrimental to the marriage and forbidden.

32.) Nabî ﷺ has stated, "The most detestable of lawful things by Allâh ﷻ is talâq (divorce)." (Abu Dâwûd) Don't abuse this responsibility of issuing talâq, given to you by Allâh ﷻ. Talâq has been allowed as a last resort after all avenues of reconciliation have been exhausted and if the marriage has broken down and there is no other way out.

33.) Never use the word 'talaaq' or 'divorce' neither in jest nor in anger. If the need arises, seek the advice of an 'alim or mufti before resorting to divorce.

34.) Exercise patience. Never make hasty decisions which you will regret later. "Allaah is with those who exercise patience."

35.) If your wife is troubled with worries or is depressed, then be sympathetic and encourage her to discuss the problem with you. Make du'a for her. Be an anchor of support and a pillar of strength for her by practically expressing your moral support. This will Insha-Allaah make her truly appreciate your heartfelt concern for her.

36.) Remember that your wife has made the great sacrifice of leaving the confines of her parent's home and her near and dear ones to come and spend the rest of her life with you- a life of the unknown. This she does with great hopes and expectations. Do not destroy them. Fulfil all these requisites which you have made binding on yourself through marriage. Appreciate and value these sacrifices. Allâh ﷻ will surely reward you in this world and the hereafter.

37.) Never demand back any gift given to your wife, even if the marriage ends in divorce. It is totally forbidden to repossess gifts given at the time of marriage or at any other time.

38.) Never allow your wife to mix with other strange men. This will severely harm your marriage. The hadith describes a man who allows his wife to talk and freely mix with other men as a 'dayyooth' (cuckold).(Ahmad) You too should abstain from talking unnecessarily to strange women.

Strange (ghair-mahram) in the shari'ah refers to all people with whom marriage is permissible in Islam. Included in these people are cousins, brothers-in-law, sisters-in-law, parent's brothers and sisters spouses, father and mother-in-law's brothers and sisters, etc. Nabi ﷺ has stated that the brother-in-law is death. The cases where an illicit relationship was established in family circles are very many and the consequences are disastrous. Never trust the nafs. Shaytân runs through the veins of man.

39.) It is your Islâmic obligation to be the breadwinner of the family. Never shirk in your responsibility and unduly burden your wife with the onerous task of supporting your family. This unnecessary strain on her will be a cause of great sorrow and lament, and you will be answerable to Allâh ﷻ in the hereafter for neglecting your fundamental duty to your family. A sign of qiyâmah is that men will bring their womenfolk into their businesses.

ETIQUETTES FOR WIVES

Nabî ﷺ has stated:
"The woman who offers her five times salah, fasts in the month of Ramadhan, protects her honour and respect, and obeys her husband has the choice of entering Jannah from whichever door she wishes to enter from." (Ibn Hibbân)
"The woman who passes away in such a state that her husband is happy with her will enter Jannah." (Tirmidhi)
"Were I to command anyone to prostrate to anyone besides Allaah ﷻ, I would have commanded the woman to prostrate to her husband. If the husband orders the wife to carry the boulders of one mountain to the next, and then to a third, she will have to do this." (Ahmad)

1.) Obey your husband in all permissible matters. This will draw the mercy of Allâh ﷻ. Nabî ﷺ said, "The best of women is she who makes her husband feel happy when he glances at her; she obeys him when he instructs her and she does not oppose him in regard to herself and her wealth by doing what he dislikes." (Hâkim)
2.) When your husband enters the home, always make salaam cheerfully and give him a warm affectionate smile, no matter how difficult your day may have been. Similarly when leaving home in the morning, make a point of kissing your husband and make salaam. Salâm is a means of engendering great love and happiness in the home.
3.) If you had a difficult or tiring day, try to appear cheerful. Do not make a point of making your husband aware as soon as he

enters the house. This could cause him to become angry. Gradually try to win his compassion and sympathy.

4.) You should abstain from all things and every form of behaviour that find disfavour with the husband. Acquaint yourself with the moods and act accordingly, to cultivate his pleasure. Do not increase his worries. Strive to become a source of comfort and peace for him,

5.) Endeavour to eat and drink from the same utensil. Sometimes place a morsel of food in each other's mouth (not only to be practised when newly-wed), this will increase mutual love. One will be rewarded for this.

6.) Keep the home, children and (most important) yourself neat and tidy when he enters the home. This will enhance his confidence in you. A neglected home could affect his mood adversely.

7.) Try to complete your household chores early and quickly so that you can spend quality time with your husband and children.

8.) Do not disclose your husband's secrets or faults to either family members or friends. Always conceal one another's faults. Even worse is to speak about one's physical relationship.

9.) Be prepared for him at meal times, as the heat of hunger is very often inflammable. Remember the adage, "A hungry man is an angry man."

10.) Do not mingle and speak to strange men. This will severely harm your marriage. Never allow any strange man to enter your house in the absence of your husband; no matter how well you or your husband knows him.

11.) It is the wife's obligatory duty to beautify and adorn herself only for her husband. It is forbidden for her to adorn herself for all and sundry, when leaving the house. A hadith states, "A woman who applies perfume and passes by a gathering is like an adulteress."

12.) Nabî ﷺ said, "It is not permissible for any woman to keep an (optional) fast without her husband's permission." (Abu Dâwûd)

13.) Never compare nor mention the handsomeness, character, wealth or generosity of other men to your husband. This is extremely insensitive and may cause jealousy, suspicion and unnecessary doubts in his mind. Accept your husband for what he is and do not cast lustful glances at other men. By doing so, shaytân will beautify the form of these other men. By controlling one's gazes, love for the husband will increase and she will attain the sweetness of iman.

14.) Do not keep in touch or communicate with any male acquaintances from the past, even if they are 'just good friends'. This is extremely detrimental to the marriage and forbidden.

15.) <u>Learn to communicate constructively.</u> Make a resolution that at the time of a problem you would sit down and discuss in a dignified manner, without raising voices or being abusive; or you will seek advice from someone you both can confide in.

16.) You cannot choose not to communicate-even your silence and body language can send important messages. However, they may be misinterpreted and could cause more harm.

17.) Misunderstandings and minor differences should not be suppressed. Rather discuss them in an amicable manner; else this could ultimately lead to a broken marriage (Allâh ﷻ save us.)

18.) If you are overcome by anger, then immediately move away from that place, drink water and recite Ta'awudh. If possible, make wudhu. Never discuss a problem in the state of anger. Calm down first.

19.) Don't ever argue in public or in front of the children. This can affect the children psychologically and could prove detrimental to the marriage.

20.) In a serious conflict, call in arbitrators from both sides and let the matter be solved amicably.

21.) Exercise patience. Never make hasty decisions which you will regret later. "Allâh is with those who exercise patience."

22.) Control your tongue at all times. One of the main reasons for breakup of marriages is the misuse of the tongue. Thereafter you will regret for the rest of your life. Nabî ﷺ said, He who keeps silent is saved." (Tirmidhi) Remember that wounds afflicted by swords may heal, but the wounds afflicted by the tongue very seldom heal.

23.) **Learn to admit your mistakes. This is a sign of humility. Do not attempt to justify your mistakes.**

24.) Nabî ﷺ said, "The woman who asks her husband for a divorce (without a valid reason), the fragrance of Jannah becomes unlawful for her." (Tirmidhi)

25.) Respect, and honour your husband's parents as your own, address them politely and treat them kindly as you would treat your own parents. For the sake of your own happiness and for the sake of your husband, it is essential to maintain a good relationship with the in-laws.

26.) Regard his family as yours. Never insult his family nor use past events or his background to hurt him. You can never acquire the love of your husband if you attempt to disrupt his relationship with his mother, father, brothers, sisters and other relatives. Disruption of family ties is amongst the worst of major sins, and invites the wrath of Allaah ﷻ.

27.) Never regard your obedience and service to your husband in mundane acts as insignificant. In fulfilling his wishes, you are obeying the command of Allâh ﷻ who has made incumbent upon you total obedience to your husband (in permissible matters). Nabî ﷺ said, "O women, look. Your husband is either your Jannah or Jahannum."

28.) The reward of a woman's activities within the confines of her home is clearly seen in the reply of Nabî ﷺ to a woman who requested to participate in jihad. Nabî ﷺ said, "Convey to any woman whom you meet, that obedience to the husband and acknowledging his rights are equal to jihad. However, few among you do so."

29.) Nabi ﷺ said, "When a woman leaves home without her husband's permission, then all the angels in the skies and entire universe curse her for this act until she returns home."

30.) Do not be demanding and imposing. This leads to serious conflicts. Learn to request politely, rather than demand.

31.) Do not feel shy to compliment your husband. Make him feel important and win him over with kind words. Adopt a cheerful appearance-this will ignite the face of even a gloomy husband. On the other hand, nagging will produce the adverse effect.

32.) Your expression of pleasure and appreciation for the 'little gifts' he brings for you will be a source of great happiness and pleasure for him.

33.) Nabî ﷺ said, "When a husband calls his wife to bed (at night for sexual relations) and she refuses (without any valid shar'i reason), then the angels curse her till the morning."

34.) Ingratitude is a common malady amongst women. Nabî ﷺ once addressing the womenfolk said that the majority of the inmates of Jahannum will be women because of their cursing in abundance and ingratitude to their husbands.

35.) Never yell at your husband, especially in public. You will hurt his ego. Do not become his mouthpiece- if he is asked a question, let him answer it himself. Do not make decisions for him, nor interrupt his discussions.

36.) If your husband is troubled with worries or is depressed, then be sympathetic and encourage him to discuss the problem with you. Make du'a for him. Be an anchor of support and a pillar of strength for him, by practically expressing your moral support. This will Insha-Allâh make him truly appreciate your heartfelt concern for him.

37.) If you require extra money, ask politely; keeping in mind his financial status. Refrain from making unreasonable and extravagant demands on him. Maintain the household budget within your means. Do not express displeasure when he is unable to fulfil your lavish demands.

38.) Learn to forgive him. Remember the English adage "To err is human, to forgive is Divine."

39.) Show him your trust and do not pry into his affairs. Do not ask too many questions. Safeguard his assets, he will have great trust in you.

A marriage, no matter how rosy it seems at the outset, will sometimes be faced with problems and difficulties, like weeds in an unattended garden. If we nip them in the bud (i.e. discuss and resolve them) when they surface, then we can foster a happy married relationship and make the bond of love stronger. However, if we ignore these initial stumbling blocks and pretend they do not exist, then they may increase and Allâh forbid, they may become so deep-rooted that attempts to remedy them later on may fail. Even if they are resolved, they could still taint the love and affection of the couple for many years to come, and make life very unpleasant.

CONCLUSION

May Allâh ﷻ accept this effort, make it a means of reviving the sunnah and a cause of everlasting rewards for all those who assisted in this publication. A special appreciation to Moulânâ Muntasiruz Zamân and Moulânâ Imraan Kajee who corrected and edited many sections of the kitâb and who provided valuable input.

BIBLIOGRAPHY

1.) Qurân Sharif
2.) Tafsir Ibn Kathîr by Hafez Imâduddin Ibn Kathir
3.) Mishkât Sharif and commentary
4.) Hayâtus Sahâbah by Moulana Muhammad Yusuf Kandehlewi (rahimahullah)
5.) Behishti Zewar by Hakimul-Ummah Moulana Ashraf Alî Thânwi (rahimahullah)
6.) Islâmi Shâdî by Hakimul-Ummah Moulana Ashraf Alî Thânwi (rahimahullah)
7.) Sirat Mustaphâ by Moulânâ Idris Kandehlewi (rahimahullah)
8.) Upbringing of children by Moulana Qamruz Zamân Saheb (dâmat barakâtuhu)
9.) Wedding Customs by Fisabilillah publications
10.) Fatâwa Darul Ulûm Zakariyya by Mufti Radhâ-ul-Haqq Saheb (dâmat barakâtuhu)

www.ingramcontent.com/pod-product-compliance
Lightning Source LLC
Chambersburg PA
CBHW051454290426
44109CB00016B/1749